Oscar Israelowitz's

Guide to
Jewish U.S.A.

Volume II — The South

ISRAELOWITZ PUBLISHING

NEW YORK   1988

Library of Congress Catalogue Card Number: 87-80153
International Standard Book Number: 0-9611036-6-3

Printed in the United States.

Cover Photos

Temple Emanu-El of Borough Park - Stained Glass Window
Cuban Hebrew Congregation - Miami Beach, Florida

Contents

INTRODUCTION

The Guide to Jewish U.S.A. is designed for the world traveller, student, and historian who has visited many ports-of-call in search of Jewish communities and yet has not had the time nor the opportunity to discover the myriads of Jewish communities and historic sites right here in their own backyard—in the U.S.A.

The guide contains brief histories of the first Jewish settlements in each state. There are listings and background stories of Jewish historic landmarks, Jewish museums, synagogues, kosher restaurants and hotels, and mikvehs.

This guide has a special feature called "The Old Neighborhoods." As the original Jewish settlers of a town or city moved away from the "Jewish" section, the old synagogues were often "left behind." The guide contains listings of hundreds of these former synagogue buildings. Some of the buildings have been demolished as the slum areas were cleared and replaced with Urban Renewal projects. Many of the former synagogues, however, are still extant, but have undergone a metamorphosis. They are now churches, day-care centers, playhouses, office complexes, or warehouses. Although the buildings have undergone a change of ownership, it is still possible to find the original Judaic symbols such as the Star of David or a cornerstone bearing the Hebrew inscriptions or the date of construction in Hebrew characters.

This guide is designed for the explorer who wishes to discover the great Jewish "treasures" that have been abandoned and forgotten by the Jewish communities. This book is also a tribute to all of the Jewish pioneers who helped establish Jewish communities throughout the United States.

A special note of thanks is due to all of the people who assisted in providing information, historical data, and photographs for this guide. There's so much to see and do in Jewish U.S.A., so let's begin.

The first Jewish settlers in America were largely Sephardic. They were descendants of those Jews who had lived in Spain and Portugal for over one thousand years but were forced, in the year 1492, either to accept Christianity or leave the country. This Spanish Inquisition was just one event in their Diaspora and their search for freedom and a peaceful existence.

In 1654, Portugal conquered Brazil and expelled the Jews living in the city of Recife. The Jews set sail in the Caribbean Sea but were captured by Spanish pirates. They were subsequently rescued and brought to New Amsterdam. Their troubles were not over yet. The governor of New Amsterdam, Peter Stuyvesant was a notorious anti-Semite. He refused to let Jews into his colony. It was not until pressure was applied by his commanding officers in Amsterdam that the first twenty three Jews were permitted to live freely in America. This was the first official Jewish settlement in North America.

For the first two centuries after their settlement in New Amsterdam, the Jewish community in America increased very slowly. By the time of the American Revolution in 1776, of a total population of three million, only some two thousand were Jews. From the Colonial period through the early 1800s, a sizable percentage of America's Jewish community assimilated into Christian society through marriage and by lapse.

Between 1820 and 1850, about 200,000 Jews arrived from the Ashkenazic countries of Germany and Bohemia. They were fleeing from political oppression and grinding poverty. It was during this period that the Reform movement developed in Europe and in the United States.

Most of these German Jews started their business careers as peddlers. They would journey out into the country, knocking on doors of isolated farmhouses and tried to sell to the farmwives a few stockings, spools of cotton thread, needles or cheap household crockery. They worked long hours and saved every penny until they could purchase a horse and wagon, or set up a small dry goods shop. This was the beginning of such great department stores as B. Altman's, Macy's, Bamberger's, Filene's, and Bloomingdale's.

The third and largest wave of immigration came between 1881 and 1925. The new arrivals were Yiddish-speaking Jews from Russia, Poland, Galicia, Roumania, and Hungary. The Russian Jews fled from their country in the wake of the bloody pogroms instigated by the Czar's government. Oppressive laws combined with the constant threat of massacre to drive the Jews of Eastern Europe from their homes in tremendous numbers. When this wave of immigration was stopped by U.S. law in 1924, the Jewish population in the United States had grown to nearly 4½ million.

The Jewish population in the United States is approximately 6,000,000.

IMPORTANT NOTE: Although every effort has been made to ensure accuracy, changes will occur after the "guide" has gone to press. Particular attention must be drawn to the fact that kosher food establishments change hands often and suddenly, in some cases going over to a non-kosher ownership. No responsiblity, therefore, can be taken for the absolute accuracy of the information, and visitors are advised to obtain confirmation of kashruth claims.

ALABAMA

The story of the Jewish community of Alabama may be traced back almost to the year 1702 when the first settlement was founded on Mobile Bay by French colonists serving under Le Moyne de Bienville. They were French and Portuguese Jews, traders, and soldiers. In 1724, Bienville promulgated the vicious "Black Code" which ordered the expulsion of all Jews from the district and sought to establish Catholicism as the only legally recognized religion. In 1763, the British seized control of the port on the Bay and showed no discrimination against the few Jews who did remain.

In 1813, General Wilkinson seized possession of Mobile in the name of the United States. Jews now filtered into the Southern Seaport. They included: Sephardic Jews who came from South America, from Amsterdam, from England, from the states to the north; immigrant Jews fleeing the repressive laws of the German states and western Poland; Jews with established business reputations; Jews with packs on their backs; a famous Jewish physician named Solomon Mordecai; a prominent lawyer from South Carolina, Philip Philips, who became the first Jew in the United States to serve as Congressman.

The first permanent Jewish settlement occurred in Mobile in the 1820s. On January 25, 1844, the first synagogue in Alabama, Congregation Shaarai Shomayim U-Maskil El Dol (Gates of Heaven and Society of the Friends of the Needy) was incorporated. Another Jewish community took root in Montgomery during the 1840s as well. Most of the Jews during that period were of German descent. Their trades varied from dry goods shopkeeper, to tailor, to tobacconist, to slave dealer.

During the Civil War there were about 130 Alabama Jews serving in the Confederate Army. Montgomery was the first capitol of the Confederacy. Judah. P. Benjamin, a native of Charleston, South Carolina, was appointed first Attorney General of the Confederacy and then Secretary of War, and Secretary of State. Rabbi Jacob Gutheim, who had closed his synagogue in New Orleans in 1862 rather than live under the Union flag, became the first rabbi of Montgomery's Congregation Kahl Montgomery.

Other Jewish communities in Alabama were organized in Huntsville (1850), Clairbourne (1855), Selma (1867), Eufala (1870), Birmingham (1882), Sheffield (1884), Demopolis (1886), Bessemer (1891), and Anniston (1893). Most of these early Jewish congregations became Reform by 1890. In the 1880s, East European immigrants established their own Orthodox, and later, Conservative synagogues.

Following World War II, there was an increase in the Jewish population in Alabama from the north. It was due to the influx of Jews who had trained during the war at Alabama army camps and airbases and came back to settle there.

During the 1950s and 1960s there was turmoil within the Jewish community throughout the Southern States. It followed the Supreme Court's decision ordering all public schools desegregated. The northern Jews were pro-integrationists and came to march with the blacks in their freedom marches. The southern Jews were fearful of attacks by the Ku Klux Klan and other radical groups. Synagogues were actually fire-bombed in Birmingham and Gasden during these years.

The Jewish population of Alabama is approximately 9,000.

Temple Emanu-El's first building was built in 1886.

BIRMINGHAM

TEMPLE EMANU-EL
2100 Highland Avenue

In June, 1870, the valley which lay at the foot of Red Mountain in Jefferson County was a wooded plain that was broken only by an occasional field of corn. Passage through the valley was provided by a few narrow roads or old Indian foot-paths. Twelve years later, in June, 1882, when Temple Emanu-El was incorporated, this same valley contained the booming industrial town of Birmingham and a burgeoning population of iron workers, coal miners, real estate speculators, and merchants. Jews were drawn by the prospect of a booming urban economy. Real estate speculators were paying dividends amounting to a 2,000 percent return on the investment. City taxes were 50 cents on each $100.

Temple Emanu-El's first synagogue was located on the corner
of Fifth Avenue and 17th Street, North. It was begun in June,
1886 and was to cost $12,000. The cornerstone ceremonies were
conducted by Rabbi Isaac Mayer Wise and Mr. Samuel Ullman,
the congregation's lay rabbi and Birmingham's civic and educational leader. Many of the city's public buildings have been named
in his honor. In 1914, Temple Emanu-El's present building was
constructed. It was designed by architect W.C. Weston in Classical
Revival style. Rabbi Morris Neufield, the congregation's rabbi
from 1895-1940, presided over the dedication. Temple Emanu-El
follows the Reform ritual.

Birmingham's Temple Emanu-El.

MOBILE

SPRING HILL AVENUE TEMPLE
(CONGREGATION SHA'ARAI SHOMAYIM)

On January 25, 1844, the first synagogue in Alabama, Congregation Shaarai Shomayim U-Maskil El Dol (Gates of Heaven and Society of the Friends of the Needy) was incorporated. On December 27, 1846, the St. Emanuel Street Temple, which had previously served as the Turnverein Hall, was dedicated. Mendes da Silva, a Sephardic scholar, became the first minister of the congregation.

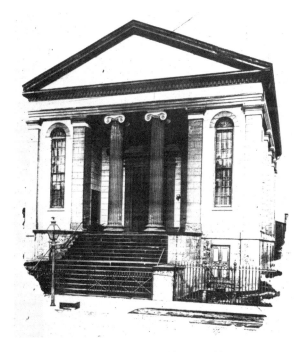

Mobile's Congregation Shaarai Shomayim.

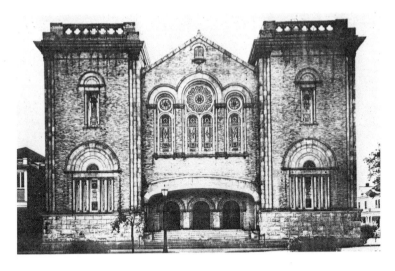

The Government Street Temple was built in 1907.

In 1853, the congregation outgrew its original building and purchased their second building on Jackson Street. That building originally housed the Unitarian Church and the Mobile Music Association. In 1870, Abraham Laser, who first served the congregation as cantor and later became rabbi, died as a martyr during the yellow fever epidemic. Knowing full well the personal danger which he was courting, he persisted in his rabbinical duties to the sick and dying until he himself fell victim of the dread disease. In recognition of his heroism the congregation erected a monument to his memory, still standing in the old Magnolia Cemetery.

In 1907, the congregation completed its new Temple on Government Street. It worshipped in that building until 1955. The present Temple on Spring Hill Avenue was designed by T. Cooper Van Antwerp and has received an award for outstanding architecture and design by the Historic Mobile Preservation Society. The congregation follows the Reform ritual.

Mobile's Springhill Avenue Temple was designed by T, Cooper Van Antwerp.

MONTGOMERY

TEMPLE BETH OR
2246 Narrow Lane Road

Abraham Mordecai of Pennsylvania was the first Jewish settler in this section of Alabama. In 1785, he located near Line Creek, about 20 miles east of Montgomery. He acquired an Indian wife, sired a large family and lived to be more than a hundred years old. He carried on a successful business trading with both white settlers and Indians. Gradually other Jews came to Alabama after the beginning of the nineteenth century. The Sick and Burial Society,

Chevre Mevacher Cholim, incorporated into Montgomery's first congregation in 1849. It changed its name to Kahl Montgomery and followed a strictly Orthodox ritual.

At the death of Judah Touro, the New Orleans philanthropist, Kahl Montgomery received, under the terms of his will, a bequest of $2,000 to be used as a nucleus of a building fund for a temple. The first temple was located at the corner of Catoma and Church Streets. It was completed in 1860 at a cost of $12,000. The threat of the Civil War was already apparent. Shortly after the temple was built the order was sent out from Montgomery to fire on Fort Sumter; Jefferson Davis was elected and took office as President of the Confederacy; and Montgomery was made, for a brief period, the capital of the seceding Southern states.

Montgomery's Temple Beth Or was built during the Civil War and was located at Church & Catoma Streets.

JOSIAH WEIL	HENRY WEIL	A. STRASSBURGER	DAVID WEIL
1852-1859	1866-1869	1869-1872	1872-1873
		1875-1877	1874-1875
			1877-1878
			1892-1919

The first Presidents of Temple Beth Or.

The war seems to have had little effect on the affairs of the growing congregation. The Jews of Montgomery were honorably represented in the Confederate Army, though some availed themselves of the privilege of "hiring a substitute" to serve in their stead.

The new synagogue was dedicated on Friday, March 8, 1862. Rabbi James K. Gutheim of New Orleans accepted the invitation to conduct services at the dedication. A radical departure from Orthodoxy was inaugurated with the installation of a choir, accompanied by music; and the conduct of part of the services in English, instead of the usual German. Other Reform customs began to creep into the services. Though the wearing of hats in temple, and the observance of stringent dietary laws in the home were not abolished. In 1874, the Reform ritual used by the Temple Emanu-El of New York was adopted. At that time the name of the temple was designated as "Beth Or."

On June 6, 1902, the second temple, located at the corner of Sayre and Clayton Streets, was built. It was designed by the architectural firm of the Stone Brothers. In 1903, it was found that the dome of the temple was unsafe and the temple was condemned for worship until repairs could be made. The congregation was awarded $9,000 in the lawsuit against the construction company.

The stained-glass windows of Temple Beth Or.

During World Wars I and II the temple was used as an entertainment and social hall for the men in uniform stationed in Montgomery. The present temple is located at 2246 Narrow Lane Road. It was dedicated in October, 1961.

Beth Or's second building was located at Sayre & Clayton Streets.

20

Alabama

SYNAGOGUES

[Note: All area codes 205]

Anniston 36201 Temple Beth El (R) *Quintard Avenue & 13th Street* 236-9249

Bessemer Temple Beth El *600 North 17th Street*

Birmingham 35205 Congregation Beth El (C) *2179 Highland Avenue South* 933-2740
Chabad Lubavitch (O) *3340 Overton Road (Mountain Brook)* 967-2202
Temple Emanu-El (R) *2100 Highland Avenue South* 933-8037
Knesseth Israel Congregation (O) *3225 Montevallo Road* 879-1664

Demopolis 36732 Temple B'nai Jeshurun (R) *406 North Main Street* 289-2378

Dothan 36301 Temple Emanu-El (R) *110 North Park Avenue* 792-5001

Florence 35630 Temple B'nai Israel (R) *210 Hawthorne Street* 764-9242

Gadsen 35902 Congregation Beth Israel (R) *761 Chestnut Street* 546-3223

Huntsville 35801 Temple B'nai Sholom (R) *103 Lincoln Street S.E.* 536-4771
Congregation Etz Chaim (C) *7705 Baily Cove Road S.E.* 881-6260

Jasper 35501 Temple Emanu-El (R) *1501 Fifth Avenue* 221-4000

Mobile   36607   Congregation Ahavas Chesed (C)   1717
Dauphin Street   476-6010
Temple Shaaray Shomayim (R)   *1769 Spring Hill Avenue*
478-0415
Montgomery   36111   Congregation Agudath Israel (C)
3525 Cloverdale Road   281-7394
Temple Beth Or (R)   *2246 Narrow Lane Road*   262-3314
Chabad Lubavitch (O)   *2820 Fairlane Drive*   277-2666
Etz Chaim Synagogue (C)   *725 Augusta Street*   281-9819
Tuscaloosa   35401   Temple Emanu-El (R)   *2320 East*
Skyland Road   553-3286

THE OLD NEIGHBORHOODS

The following list contains information about synagogues which
are no longer functioning as Jewish houses of worship. These
addresses are located in the old sections of the city or town. It is
advisable to take extra precautions while driving through these
neighborhoods.

Anniston   Temple Beth El   *1029 Noble Street*
Birmingham   Temple Emanu-El   *Fifth Avenue & 17th*
Street North
Knesseth Israel Congregation   *22nd Street, between 5th and*
6th Avenues   *1700 7th Avenue North*
Demopolis   Temple B'nai Jeshurun   *340 Drawer Street*
Eufala   Congregation B'nai Israel   *Barbour Street*
Huntsville   Temple B'nai Sholom   *Lincoln & Clinton Streets*
Congregation Etz Chaim   *2501 Whitesburg Drive, South*

Lanette   Temple Beth El

Mobile   Congregation Ahavas Chesed   *557 Conti Street*
Temple Shaaray Shomayim   *Jackson Street*
Government Street

Montgomery   Congregation Aguudath Israel   *507 South McDonough Street*
Temple Beth Or   *Catoma & Church Streets·*
109 Clayton Street

Selma   Congregation Mishkan Israel   *503 Broad Street*

Sheffield   Tri-Cities Jewish Congregation   *Atlantic Avenue & 8th Street*

Tuscaloosa   Temple Emanu-El   *1208 10th Street*

Uniontown   *B'nai Israel Congregation*

ARKANSAS

The first *minyan* in Arkansas was organized in 1845 in Little Rock. It was not until 1866, however, that Temple B'nai Israel was established. One of the leaders of the first Jewish community in Little Rock was Jonas Levy. He became mayor of Little Rock in 1860. He was the city's Chief Executive during the Civil War while the city was occupied by the Union Army.

Before the Civil War, there were Jewish settlements in Fort Smith, Pine Bluff, DeValls Bluff, Van Buren, Jonesboro, and Batesville. Fort Smith and Van Buren became key starting points in 1849 for pioneers taking the Southern route to the Gold Rush state of California. The Adler family would journey to New York and Philadelphia once a year for Rosh Hashana. Samuel Adler owned a cotton plantation. While in Philadelphia, he learned the elementary practice of *shechitah*, ritual slaughter, so that his family could observe the dietary laws out in the frontier town of Van Buren, Arkansas.

Following the Civil War, a considerable number of Jewish merchants, planters, and shopkeepers began moving into the river towns as well as to Hot Springs and Little Rock. As Arkansas slowly recovered from the chaos of war and Reconstruction, Jewish enterprise played a considerable role in establishing saw mills, railroads, and small industries. At one time there were 14 towns and villages named for and founded by Jews in the postwar period. Some of the names include Altheimer, Berger, Bertig, Felsenthal, Goldman, Levy, and Weiner.

Some early Jewish congregations in Arkansas were organized in Hot Springs (1878), Fort Smith (1881), Texarkan (1884), Jonesboro (1897), Newport (1905), Eudora (1912), and Forest City (1904). The Jewish population of Arkansas is approximately 3,300.

LITTLE ROCK

CONGREGATION B'NAI ISRAEL
3700 Rodney Parham

Congregation B'nai Israel was officially organized on November 11, 1866, by a group of Jewish veterans of the Civil War. The first sanctuary, a small room in the Ditter Building between Rock and Cumberland Streets on East Markham, was dedicated on August 13, 1867.

The congregation also soon provided for necessary social services. The Ladies Benevolent Society, the congregation's first Jewish women's organization was organized in 1867 as an adjunct to both serve the congregation and dispense charity to the needy and suffering, not only Little Rock but throughout the South.

The congregation's second synagogue was a brick structure erected on Center Street between 3rd and 4th Streets at a cost of $7,000. There was a Sabbath School called Talmud Yelodim Institute which served an average of 55 children.

B'nai Israel was one of the 32 charter congregations of the Union of American Hebrew Congregations, the parent organization of Reform Judaism in America. From its beginning, B'nai Israel has grown to become recognized as one of the leading Reform Jewish congregations in the South. Congregation members have served in the Arkansas Legislature, on boards of numerous colleges and universities, and in the nation's armed forces during both World Wars.

The congregation celebrated its 100th anniversary in 1966 in its venerable sanctuary at Capitol Street and Broadway, a building that was a distinguished Little Rock landmark for almost eight decades. Congregation B'nai Israel membership consists of over 400 families.

SYNAGOGUES

[Note: All area codes 501]

Fayetteville   72701   Temple Sholom (R)   607 *Storer Street*
521-7357

Fort Smith   72901   United Hebrew Congregation (R)
126 North 47th Street   452-1468

Helena   72342   Temple Beth El (R)   406 *Perry Street*
338-6654

Hot Springs   71901   Congregation Beth Jacob (O)
200 Quapaw Avenue   623-9335
Congregation House of Israel (R)   300 *Quapaw Avenue*
623-5821

Little Rock   72205   Congregation Agudath Achim (O)
7901 West 5th Street   225-1683
Temple B'nai Israel (R)   3700 *Rodney Parham Road*
225-9700

McGhee   71654   Temple Meier Chayim (R)   210 *North 4th*
Street   222-4399

Pine Bluff   71601   Temple Anshe Emeth (R)   40th &
Hickory Streets   534-3853

THE OLD NEIGHBORHOODS

The following list contains information about synagogues which are no longer functioning as Jewish houses of worship. These addresses are located in the old sections of the city or town. It is advisable to take extra precautions while driving through these neighborhoods.

Blytheville   Temple Israel   *1500 Heorn Street*

El Dorado   Temple Beth Israel   *712 Camp Street*

Camden   United Hebrew Congregation   *11th & East Streets*

Fort Smith   United Hebrew Congregation   *422 North 11th Street*

Hot Springs   Congregation House of Israel   *1879 Quapaw Avenue   Central Avenue, between Olive & Orange Streets*

Jonesboro   Temple Israel   *203 West Oak Street Main Street*

Little Rock   Congregation Agudath Achim   *801 Louisiana Avenue*
Temple B'nai Israel   Capitol Avenue & Broadway
East Markham, between Rock & Cumberland Streets
Center, between 3rd & 4th Streets

Pine Bluff   Temple Anshe Emeth   *Poplar & 2nd Streets*

FLORIDA

One of the most prominent Florida pioneers at the beginning of the American period in 1821 was Moses Elias Levy. He had migrated from Morocco in North Africa to the Virgin Islands and then to Cuba. In the last days of the Spanish era in Florida he acquired an extensive land grant in present-day Alachua County. He planned to establish a colony of Orthodox Jews on the land, perhaps to make an American refuge for them. He secured United States citizenship for himself and his family at the time of the change of flags, and the United States recognized the validity of his land claims.

His son David served as territorial delegate to the Congress of the United States and participated in the convention that drafted Florida's first state constitution. David Levy was a principal promoter of statehood, which was achieved in 1845, and he became one of Florida's first two United States senators, the first Jew to sit in that body. In the same year his name became David Levy Yulee by act of the state legislature. He became a major producer of sugar on a plantation near Homosassa and went on to organize the company that built Florida's first cross-state railroad, from Fernandina to Cedar Key.

The success of the Yulee family was not accompanied by any considerable migration of Jews to the state. The first Jewish community in Florida was established in the 1850s at Jacksonville, the state's commercial metropolis and railroad center. The first religious services were held during the Civil War period in Jacksonville and Pensacola. Tampa's first congregation, Shaai Zedek, was organized in 1894.

The largest city in Florida in the 1880s was Key West. Joe Wolfson landed there by chance in 1884 when his ship was wrecked

David Levy Yulee was Florida's first senator.

on the Florida Reef. He liked the place well enough to induce his family to join him. Others soon followed them. Practically all the Jews in Key West became peddlers. They soon became merchants of dry goods and clothing. Some went into groceries and furniture.

The first synagogue in Key West, Rodef Sholom, was organized in 1896. At first they met on the second floor of Louis Fine's furniture store. In 1905, they purchased what had been the home of Dr. John B. Maloney and converted it into a synagogue, possibly the only one in the United States with a widow's walk on top. For a time the congregation split into two groups, the second taking the name of B'nai Zion. They soon reconciled their differences, however, and Conservative B'nai Zion has since been the only congregation in Key West.

In 1912, the first train reached Key West over the Florida East Coast Railway Company's extension to the island. On Labor Day of 1935 a hurricane destroyed much of the tracks, bridges, causeways, and rolling stock. The Florida Highway Department acquired the property and constructed on the right-of-way the present Overseas Highway to Key West.

When the Florida East Coast Railroad began to be pushed southward in the latter part of the nineteenth century, enterprising Jewish businessmen followed its progress southward. They set up shops and offices in Fort Pierce, West Palm Beach, and Miami. The first Jewish residents in Miami were Samuel Singer and Isidor Cohen who opened dry goods stores near the railroad terminus.

The first synagogue in Miami was organized in 1912 as Congregation B'nai Zion. In 1917, it was reorganized and received its charter as Temple Beth David. They purchased the former First Christian Church located at Avenue H and 10th Street and refurbished it for use as Miami's first synagogue. Temple Beth David began as a Conservative congregation, but strong Orthodox elements were in it. The first to pull out, though, were supporters of the Reform interpretation of Judaism who founded Temple Israel in 1922. The Orthodox group was organized as the Miami Orthodox Congregation in 1931, later as the Miami Hebrew Congregation, and finally as Temple Beth El. In 1926, a different Orthodox group had organized a congregation in Miami Beach which took the name Beth Jacob and acquired a synagogue on Washington Avenue and 3rd Street.

Temple Israel built its first temporary synagogue structure in 1924 at 12th Avenue and 4th Street. Its present site is at 137 N.E. 19th Street. The main Sanctuary was dedicated in 1928. The complex of the temple consists of a religious school and auditorium and its most recent addition, the unique Gumenick Chapel. There is a suburban branch of this congregation located in Kendall.

Miami Beach was at first almost exclusively developed by Gentiles, and the sales appeal was primarily to them. The earliest hotels were restricted to white Gentiles. The first Jewish hotels were the Sea Breeze and Nemo, both built within two blocks of Beth Jacob's first synagogue. Every beach front hotel was barred to Jews until the early 1940s. Following World War II, however, Miami Beach had become an almost all-Jewish winter resort. During World War II, the Air Force requisitioned most of the hotels south of 23rd Street and converted them into barracks housing personnel undergoing officer training. Today, this area, known as the South Beach, is the site of the older hotels and rooming houses.

The South Beach section has recently been declared a National Historic District with its rich collection of Art Deco and Art Moderne hotels and residences. They are now being restored to their original elegance. This is an up-and-coming area with new chic cafes, boutiques, and discos along Ocean Drive and Collins Avenue, near 7th Street.

Following Fidel Castro's takeover of Cuba in 1959, several thousand Cuban Jews escaped to Miami Beach. They established Cuban Hebrew congregations, community centers, and cultural and benevolent societies.

The Jewish population of Florida is approximately 390,000 of which about 255,000 reside in the Greater Miami area.

Louis Wolfson's store in Key West, 1904. It was later razed to make way for the La Concha Hotel.

Smith's Casino in Miami Beach (ca. 1922) was located at the end of Collin's Bridge.

Cromer-Cassel's New York Department Store on Miami Avenue and Northeast First Street, 1925.

Aeriel view of Miami Beach, 1920.

JACKSONVILLE

CONGREGATION AHAVATH CHESED
8727 San Jose Boulevard

The first Jewish settlers in Jacksonville in the 1850s were merchants who established their businesses along Bay Street. By 1880, Jacksonville had become a thriving tourist city. The steamship lines entered the port to discharge their passengers for lengthy visits in many of the city's fine hotels, or for continued trips down the St. Johns River. Visitors shopped the bazaars and stores on Bay Street. They dined on continental cuisine in the many fashionable hotels, listened to orchestras that played nightly and attended opera, theater, prize fights and races.

It was in this bustling atmosphere that Jewish life took form. The Hebrew Benevolent Society, the B'nai Brith chapter, and the Young Men's Hebrew Literary Association were organized during this period. Religious services were held in Odd Fellows Hall at Market and Adams Streets, and in various homes.

On January 19, 1882, a group of Jewish citizens organized Jacksonville's first synagogue, Congregation Ahavath Chesed. The first president of the congregation was Morris Dzialynski. The first synagogue building was located at Laura and Union Streets. It was dedicated by its first rabbi, Marx Moses, on September 8, 1882.

The architectural style of the synagogue reflected the European origins of the membership, most of whom came from Prussia and Germany. Two oriental domes lifted their tapered points heavenward on the front of the building. Three full swinging doors opened into a vestibule which led to the Sanctuary. Inside there were 28 seats in two rows of pews giving three aisles and a seating capacity of four hundred. The seats were maple, with a framework of ash and mountings of black walnut. Overhead hung chandeliers with a central corona of 36 gas jets. The synagogues cost $7,000 and

there were 24 members. In keeping with the European Orthodox
practices, some traditions were maintained in the early days of the
congregation. Males covered their heads and wore talliths (prayer
shawls); Hebrew was used extensively in the service, the Sabbath
was strictly observed and stores were closed on High Holy Days.

Winds of Reform Judaism stirred early, and Jacob D. Bucky
consented to be president of the congregation in 1886 on condition
that the congregation would accept many of the new reforms.
Organ music had been introduced into the service as early as 1885.
Biographers record that Frederick Delius, the lyrical English com-
poser, served as organist-cantor in the synagogue for a brief period.
Delius' biographer, Arthur Hutchins, states, "Delius eked out a
living by singing in the choir and playing the organ at the synagogue,

Jacksonville's first Synagogue, Temple Ahavath Chesed.

the good Rabbi (Moses) thinking perhaps that his name was of Dutch or German-Jewish origin.''

The pogroms of the 1880s and 1890s in Russia and Poland brought the first wave of Eastern European Jews to America. A small contingent arrived in Jacksonville from Pushalot, Poland and formed the nucleus of the Orthodox Jewish community.

The Prussian and German Jews, now united in Temple Ahavath Chesed, while maintaining their identity as Jews, sought to be integrated into the larger American community. The Polish and Russian Jews, having been denied educational and civil rights, maintained strong religious ties. In 1901, B'nai Israel, an Orthodox congregation, was worshipping in the LaVilla section, an area touching both sides of Broad Street north of Bay Street.

Ahavath Chesed's 1910 building.

On May 3, 1901, sparks from a matress factory in LaVilla ignited a fire; by the time the flames were extinguished eight hours later, the fire swept an area covering 146 city blocks. Every public building except the U.S. Government Building was burned, including all city records. Twenty-three churches and ten major hotels were destroyed including Temple Ahavath Chesed and all congregational records. On April 8, 1902, less than a year after Jacksonville had been levelled by fire, the congregation moved into its rebuilt synagogue. It was a replica of the first structure.

The congregation constructed its third house of worship in 1910. It was located at the corner of Laura and Union Streets. It was designed by architect Henry J. Klutho in the Greek Revival style. The synagogue measured 105 by 60 feet, constructed of buff brick with ornamental terra-cotta trimmings. Seating capacity on the main floor was five hundred with two hundred additional seats in the balcony. The congregation remained at this location until 1950.

The next synagogue building was located at St. Johns Avenue and Mallory Street. The architectural firm was Kemp, Bunch and Jackson. In 1979, the present synagogue was dedicated. It was designed by architects Gunn and Mayerhoof. It is located at 8727 San Jose Boulevard. The congregation follows the Reform ritual.

MIAMI

TEMPLE ISRAEL
137 N.E. 19th Street

Temple Beth David, Miami's first congregation, was organized in 1912. It began as a Conservative congregation, but strong Orthodox elements were in it. The first to pull out, though, were supporters of the Reform Movement who founded Temple Israel in 1922. The first synagogue was dedicated in 1924 and was located at S.W. 12th Avenue and 4th Street. In 1928, the present temple was built. Today, there are four buildings in the Temple Israel complex: the Sam C. Levinson Community House, the Main Sanctuary, the

Miami's first synagogue, Temple Beth David, was organized in 1912.

The Gumenick Chapel in Temple Israel of Miami.

Colman A. Zwitman Religious School, and the Gumenick Chapel with the Morris D. Wolfson Auditorium.

The most recent, and for some the most controversial, building is the Gumenick Chapel, dedicated on April 13, 1969. Adjoining other temple buildings on the east, on the site of the Biblical gardens, it was designed by Kenneth Treister, who was confirmed at Temple Israel. The chapel is a striking example of the dramatic and even radical revolution in religious architecture in the United States in recent decades. The chapel has been characterized variously. Some perplexed and shocked by the unusual design referred to it in somewhat derisive terms as the concrete-colored bulge on N.E. 19th Street, a big stone igloo with holes chopped in it, a flintstone monstrosity, and Joe's cave.

The architect and his supporters explain that they have transformed religious architecture into modern forms and ancient symbols have been presented in contemporary materials and forms. Examples are Sabbath inscribed on candelabra, a bust of Moses, a modern burning bush, and a Menorah lamp burning outside a temple. The Ark consists of a free-form bronze sculpture of the *burning bush* with two exposed Torahs set inside. Another feature of the chapel are the twelve, three dimensional, stained-glass windows made for it in Belgium.

BETH DAVID CONGREGATION
2625 S.W. 3rd Avenue

The oldest congregation in Greater Miami was organized as B'nai-Zion in 1912. Its first building was the former First Christian Church, located at Avenue H and 10th Street. It started as a Conservative congregation. Offshoots from this congregation include Temple Israel (Reform) and the Miami Hebrew Congregation (Orthodox), which became Temple Beth El. B'nai Zion changed its name to Beth David in 1917. The present building was built in 1949.

MIAMI BEACH

BETH JACOB CONGREGATION
311 Washington Avenue

The first synagogue in Miami Beach was the Beth Jacob Congregation. It was built in 1929. That structure is presently used as the social hall and daily chapel for the congregation. It has recently been declared a National Historic Landmark. The corner synagogue building, with its Art Deco details, was constructed in the mid 1930s. It is used only on the major Jewish holidays and for special occasions.

TEMPLE EMANU-EL
1701 Washington Avenue

The massive domed Temple Emanu-El, located opposite the Miami Beach Convention Center, was built in 1948. It was designed by Morris, Lapidus, Liebman, & Associates. The congregation follows the Conservative ritual.

CUBAN HEBREW CONGREGATION
1700 Michigan Avenue

The Jewish community in Cuba before 1959 consisted of two distinct groups. The Ashkenazic group stemmed from Lithuania and spoke Yiddish as its mother tongue. The Sephardic group stemmed from Turkey and spoke Ladino. Both groups arrived in Havana in the early 1920s, after the United States closed its doors to all immigration. They were glad to be welcomed by the Cuban government. The Jews settled in the poor section of Havana, near the ports. They eventually worked their way up the social and

Cuban Hebrew Congregation of Miami Beach.

economic ladders and became prominent and very proud citizens of Cuba.

All this changed in 1959 when Fidel Castro took control of the government and created a Communist state. Many thousands of Jews fled Cuba at that time and settled in Miami Beach, Florida. When they arrived, the existing Jewish community did not greet these Jewish Cuban refugees with open arms. The Cuban Jews had to start their lives all over again. They first settled in the poor South Beach section of Miami Beach. Over the years they developed their closely-knit Cuban Jewish community. Today, the Cuban Jews are, for the most part, prosperous.

Before the migration of the Jewish community, there were five large synagogues in Havana. Three of these synagogues were taken over by the government and converted into Communist Party community centers. There are still about one thousand Jews living in Cuba. Those who could, left the country in the late 1950s. Some

Jews in prominent positions before the Communist takeover were not permitted to leave the country, since they were security risks. Several years ago, when hundreds of criminals from Cuban jails and mental institutions were released and shipped to Florida on the infamous "Flotilla," a number of prominent Jews were smuggled out, with the assistance of the HIAS.

Today, there are several thousand Cuban Jews living in the Greater Miami area. The largest synagogues are Temple Moses, located at 1200 Normandy Drive and the Cuban Hebrew Congregation (Congregation Beth Shmuel), located at 1700 Michigan Avenue. Both are located in Miami Beach.

The Cuban Hebrew Congregation was organized in 1961 and was first located in a store-front along Washington Avenue. In 1981, the congregation commissioned a Cuban-born Jewish architect, Oscar Sklar, to design its new synagogue. The architect used poured-concrete, designed with twelve amorphous cut-outs in its front facade. The twelve shapes are symbolic of the twelve tribes of Israel. Each cut-out contains a stained-glass window. As you enter through the doors of the two street-level cut-outs into the lobby, you can proceed directly into the main Sanctuary or you can take the elevator upstairs to the grand ballroom. The elevator's back wall is designed with a clear plate of glass. As the elevator rises, you can see the exposed stained-glass windows of the front facade.

In the main Sanctuary there are three flags, on either side of the Ark. The flag of Israel is on one side and the flags of the United States and of Cuba are on the other side. Please note that the Cuban flag has not been changed with the present Communist regime. There are 750 member families in the Cuban Hebrew Congregation. The congregation follows the Conservative ritual. The congregants in this synagogue converse in English, Spanish, and Yiddish. This is the Ashkenazic group of Cuban Jews. The Sephardic Cuban congregations in Miami Beach follow the Orthodox ritual.

SYNAGOGUES

Boca Raton 33432 Temple Beth El (R) *333 SW 4th Avenue (305) 391-8900*
B'nai Torah Congregation *1401 NW 4th Avenue 392-8566*
Temple Eternal Light (Rec.) *499 NW 13th Street 391-1111*
Congregation Beth Ami (C) *P.O.Box 7105 994-8693*
Temple Beth Shalom (C) *483-5557*
Congregation B'nai Israel (R) *22455 Boca Rio Road 483-9982*
Boca Raton Synagogue (O) *7900 Montoya Circle 394-5732*
Congregation Torah Ohr (O) *483-3960*
Boynton Beach Congregation Beth Kodesh (C) *501 N.E. 26th Avenue (305) 586-9428*
Temple Torah (C) *736-7687*
Bradenton Temple Beth El (C) *2209 75th Street, West (813) 792-0870*
Cape Coral 33904 Temple Beth El (R) *2721 Del Prado Boulevard (813) 574-5115*
Temple Beth Sholom (R) *702 S.E. 24th Avenue 772-4555*
Clearwater 33515 Congregation Beth Sholom (C) *1325 South Belcher Road (813) 531-1418*
Temple B'nai Israel (R) *1685 South Belcher Road 531-5829*
Coconut Creek Liberal Temple (R) *3950 Coconut Creek Parkway (305) 973-7494*
Conservative Synagogue of Coconut Creek (C) *1447 Lyons Road 975-4666*
Coral Gables 33146 Temple Judea (R) *5500 Granada Boulevard (305) 667-5657*
Temple Zamora (C) *44 Zamora Avenue 448-7132*
Coral Springs 33065 Temple Beth Orr (R) *2151 Riverside Drive (305) 753-3232*
Congregation B'nai Israel (C) *4129 N.W. 88th Avenue*
Chabad-Lubavitch (O) *9791 West Sample Road 344-4855*

Daytona Beach   32018   Temple Israel (C)   *1400 South Peninsula Drive*   (904) 252-3097

Deerfield Beach   Temple Beth Israel (C)   *200 S. Century Boulevard*   (305) 421-7060
Temple B'nai Sholom (R)   *2305 West Hillsboro Boulevard*   428-3307
Young Israel (O)   *1880 West Hillsboro Boulevard*   421-1367

Delray Beach   Congregation Anshei Emunah (O)   *16189 Carter Road*   (305) 499-9229
Congregation Anshei Sholom (C)   *7099 West Atlantic Avenue*   495-1300
Temple Emeth (C)   *5780 West Atlantic Avenue*   498-3536
Temple Sinai (R)   *2475 West Atlantic Avenue*   276-6161

Deltona   32763   Temple Israel (C)   *1001 East New York Avenue*   (904) 763-1646
Temple Sholom (R)   *1785 Elkcam Boulevard*   789-2202

Fort Lauderdale   33313   Temple Beth Israel (C)   *7100 West Oakland Park Boulevard*   (305) 742-4040
Temple Emanu-El (R)   *3245 West Oakland Park Boulevard*   731-2310
Temple Bat Yam (R)   *5151 N.E. 14th Terrace*   928-0410

Fort Myers   Temple Judea (C)   *14486 A&W Bulb Road*   (813) 433-0201

Fort Pierce   33450   Temple Beth El (R)   *4600 Oleander Avenue*   (305) 461-7428

Gainesvillle   Temple B'nai Israel (C)   *3830 N.W. 16th Boulevard*   (904) 376-1508

Gulfport   33707   Congregation Beth Sholom (C)   *1854 54th Street, South* (813) 321-3388

Hallandale   Jewish Center (C)   *416 N.E. 8th Avenue*   (305) 454-9100
Congregation Levi Yitzchok (O)   *1295 East Hallandale Beach Boulevard*   458-1877

Hialeah   33910   Temple Tifereth Jacob (C)   *951 East 4th Avenue*   *(305) 877-9595*

Hollywood   33020   Temple Beth Ahm (C)   *9730 Stirling Road*   *(305) 431-5100*
Temple Beth El (R)   *1351 South 14th Street*   *920-8225*
Temple Beth Sholom (C)   *1400 North 46th Avenue*   *981-6111*
Temple Sinai (C)   *1201 Johnson Street*   *920-1577*
Temple Solel (R)   *5100 Sheriden Street*   *989-0205*
Young Israel (O)   *3291 Stirling Road*   *966-7877*

Homestead   33023   Homestead Jewish Center   *183 N.E. 8th Street*

Jacksonville   32217   Temple Ahavath Chesed (R)   *8727 San Jose Boulevard*   *(904) 733-7078*
Beth Sholom Synagogue (C)   *4072 Sunbeam Road*   *268-0404*
Eitz Chaim Synagogue (O)   *5864 University Boulevard, West*   *733-0720*
Jacksonville Jewish Center (C)   *3662 Crown Point Road*   *268-6736*

Jupiter   Reform Temple of Jupiter (R)   *759 Parkway Street*   *(305) 747-1109*

Key West   B'nai Zion Congregation (C)   *750 United Street*   *(305) 294-3437*

Lakeland   33803   Temple Emanu-El (C)   *730 Lake Hollingsworth Drive*   *(813) 682-8616*

Lake Worth   33460   Temple Beth Sholom (C)   *315 North A Street*   *(305) 585-5020*
Lake Worth Jewish Center (C)   *165 Ohio Road*   *478-4720*

Lauderdale Lakes   Temple Ohel B'nai Raphael (O)   *4351 West Oakland Park Boulevard*   *733-7684*

Lauderhill   Hebrew Congregation (C)   *2048 N.W. 49th Avenue*   *(305) 733-9560*
Synagogue of Inverray-Chabad (O)   *4561 North University Drive*   *748-1777*
Temple Ohel B'nai Raphael (O)   *733-7684*

Long Boat Key   Temple Beth Israel (R)   *567 Bay Isles Road*
(813) 383-3428

Long Wood   Congregation Beth Am (C)   *1061 Alameda Drive*
(305) 834-8235

Margate   33063   Temple Beth Am (C)   *7205 Royal Palm*
Boulevard   *(305) 974-8650*
Congregation Beth Hillel (C)   *7638 Margate Boulevard*
974-3090

Merrit Island   32952   Temple Israel (R)   *1900 South*
Tropical Trail   *(305) 453-5144*

Miami   33129

Temple Beth Am (R)   *5950 North Kendall Drive   667-6667*
Temple Beth Or (Rec)   *9450 Sunset Drive   596-4523*
Temple Shir Ami (R)   *Sunset Drive & S.W. 125th Avenue*
253-9666
Shaare Tefilah Torah Center of Kendall (O)   *7880 S.W. 112th*
Street   232-6833
Bet Shira Congregation (C)   *7500 S.W. 120th Street*
238-2601
Havurah of South Florida (Rec)   *9315 S.W. 61st Street*
666-7349
Congregation Ahavas Israel (C)   *525 78th Street S.W.*
Ahavath Sholom Congregation (O)   *985 S.W. 67th Avenue*
261-5479
Congregation Bet Breira (R)   *9400 S.W. 87th Avenue*
595-1500
Beth David Congregation (C)   *2625 S.W. 3rd Avenue*
854-3911
Beth David Congregation (C)   *7500 N.W. 120th Street*
238-2601
Congregation Beth Kodesh (C)   *1101 S.W. 12th Avenue*
858-6334
Temple Beth Tov (C)   *6438 S.W. 8th Street   261-9821*
B'nai Israel Congregation (O)   *16260 S.W. 288th Street*
245-8594

Congregation B'nai Raphael   1401 N.W. 183rd Street
Chabad of Kendall   (O)   14096 S.W. 84th Street
387-3444
Havurah of South Florida (Rec.)   1100 Stanford Drive
666-7349
Temple Israel (R)   9990 North Kendall Drive   595-5055
Temple Israel of Greater Miami (R)   137 N.E. 19th Street
573-5900
Congregation of Kendall (C)   8900 S.W. 107th Avenue
Metropolitan Community Synagogue   19094 West Dixie
Highway   931-9318
Temple Samuel (C)   9353 S.W. 152nd Street   382-3668
Congregation Shaare Tefillah of Kendall (O)   15410 S.W. 75th
Circle Lane   382-1898
Temple Sinai of North Dade   18801 N.E. 22nd Avenue
932-9010
Young Israel of Greater Miami (O)   990 N.E. 171st Street
651-3591
Young Israel of Skylake (O)   1850 N.E. 183rd Street
945-8712
Temple Zion (C)   8000 Miller Road   271-2311
Miami Beach   33141   Agudath Israel Hebrew Institute (O)
7801 Carlyle Avenue
Temple Beth El (O)   2400 Pinetree Drive   532-6421
Beth Israel Congregation (O)   770 40th Street   538-1251
Beth Jacob Congregation (O)   311 Washington Avenue
672-6150
Beth Tfilah Congregation (O)   935 Euclid Avenue   538-1521
Beth Torah (C)   1051 North Miami Beach Boulevard
North Miami Beach   947-7528
Chabad of North Dade (O)   2590 N.E. 202nd Street
932-7770
Jacob Cohen Community Synagogue (O)   1532 Washington
Avenue   534-0271

Cuban Hebrew Congregation (C)   *1700 Michigan Avenue*
534-7213
1701 Lenox Avenue   673-9572
Temple Emanu-El (C)   *1701 Washington Avenue   538-2503*
King Solomon Temple (C)   *910 Lincoln Road   534-9776*
Kneseth Israel Congregation   *1415 Euclid Avenue   538-2741*
Congregation Lubavitch (O)   *1120 Collins Avenue   673-5755*
Temple Menorah (C)   *620 75th Street   866-0221*
Temple Ner Tamid (C)   *7902 Carlisle Avenue   866-8345*
North Bay Village Jewish Center (C)   *1720 79th Street*
Causeway
Congregation Ohev Shalom (O)   *7055 Bonita Drive   865-9851*
Congregation Ohr Chaim   *317 West 47th Street   674-1326*
Sephardic Jewish Center (T)   *645 Collins Avenue   534-4092*
17100 N.E. 6th Avenue
Shaaray Tefilah Congregation (O)   *991 N.E. 172nd Street*
651-8348
West Avenue Jewish Center (O)   *1140 Alton Road   673-1124*
Young Israel of Sunny Isles (O)   *17274 Collins Avenue*
949-7475
Keter Abraham Synagogue (O)   Castle Premier Hotel,
5445 Collins Avenue
Bal Harbour Synagogue (O)   *9540 Collins Avenue   868-1411*
Congregation Beit Medrash Levi Yitzchok (O)   *1140 Alton Road*
Temple Beth Raphael   *1545 Jefferson Avenue   538-4112*
Temple Beth Sholom (R)   *4144 Chase Avenue   538-7231*
Temple B'nai Zion (C)   *200 178th Street (Sunny Isles)*
932-2159
Congregation Lubavitch (O)   *1120 Collins Avenue*
Congregation Lubavitch (O)   *4130 Collins Avenue*

Miramer   33023   Temple Israel (C)   *6920 S.W. 35th Street*
(305) 961-1700
Naples   Temple Sholom (R)   *1575 Pine Ridge Road*
(813) 597-8158
North Bay Village
Temple Beth El (C)   *7800 Hispanola Avenue   861-4005*

North Miami Beach

B'nai Sephardim of Greater Miami (O)   *17495 N.E. 6th Avenue* 653-5133

Etz Chaim Congregation (O)   *1544 Washington Avenue* 531-8145

Congregation Magen David (C)   *17100 N.E. 6th Avenue* 652-2099

Gold Coast Synagogue (C)   Seacoast Towers East,   *5151 Collins Avenue*   864-8620

Temple Sinai of North Dade (C)   *18801 N.E. 22nd Avenue* 932-9010

Sephardic Jewish Center   17100 N.E. 6th Avenue   652-2099

Temple Adath Jeshurun   *1025 N.E. Miami Gardens Drive* 947-1435

Agudath Achim Congregation   *19255 N.E. 3rd Avenue* (305) 651-5392

Aventura Jewish Center (C)   *2972 Aventura Boulevard* 935-0666

Congregation Beth Moshe (C)   *2225 N.E. 121st Street* 801-5508

North Port   North Port Jewish Center (C)   *Biscayne Boulevard*   (813) 426-9048

Ocala   Temple Beth Sholom (R)   *1109 N.E. 8th Avenue* (904) 629-3587

Temple B'nai Daron (C)   *Banyan Road & Banyan Course* (904) 687-1733

Orlando   32810   Temple Israel (C)   *4917 Eli Street* (305) 647-3055

Congregation of Liberal Judaism (R)   *928 Malone Drive* 645-0444

Congregation Ohev Sholom (C)   *5015 Goddard Avenue* 298-4650

Ormond Beach   Temple Beth El (R)   *579 North Nova Road* (904) 677-2484

Palm Beach   33480   Temple Emanu-El (C)   *190 North County Road*   *(305) 832-0804*

Palm Beach Gardens   Temple Beth David (C)   *4657 Hood Road*   *(305) 694-2350*

Palm Coast   Temple Beth Sholom   *Wellington Drive* *(904) 445-3664*

Palm Springs   Temple B'nai Jacob (C)   *433-5957*

Pembroke Pines   Temple Beth Am (C)   *9730 Stirling Road* *(305) 431-5100*

Temple Beth Emet (R)   *10801 Pembroke Road*   *431-3638*

Pensacola   32501   Temple Beth El (R)   *800 North Palafox Street*   *(904) 438-3321*
Congregation B'nai Israel (C)   *1829 North 9th Avenue* *433-7311*

Plantation   Temple Kol Ami (R)   *8200 Peters Road* *(305) 472-1988*
Congregation Ramat Sholom (Rec.)   *11301 West Broward Boulevard*   *472-3600*

Pompano Beach   33060   Temple B'nai Moshe (C) *1434 S.E. 3rd Street*   *(305) 942-5380*
Temple Sholom (C)   *132 S.E. 11th Avenue*   *942-6410*

Port Charlottte   Temple Sholom (R)   *Utica Avenue & Sherwood Road*   *(813) 625-3116*

Port St. Lucie   Congregation Beth Israel (R)   *1592 Floresta Drive*   *(305) 879-1879*

Royal Palm Beach   Temple Beth Zion (C)   *798-8888*

St. Augustine   Congregation Sons of Israel (C)   *163 Cordova Street*   *(904) 829-9532*

St. Petersburg   33710   Temple Beth El (R)   *400 South Pasadena Avenue*   *(813) 347-6136*
Congregation B'nai Israel (C)   *301 59th Street, North* *381-4900*

Sarasota 33577 Temple Beth Sholom (C) *1050 South Tuttle Avenue (813) 955-8121*
Temple Emanu-El (R) *151 South McIntosh Road 371-2788*
Satellite Beach 32937 Temple Beth Sholom (C) *N.E. 3rd Street (305) 773-3039*
Seminole Congregation Beth Chai (C) *8400 125th Street, North (813) 393-5525*
Stuart Treasure Coast Jewish Center (C) *3257 S.E. Salerno Road (305) 287-8833*
Sunrise Temple Beth Israel (C) *7100 West Oakland Park Boulevard (305) 742-4040*
Temple Shaarai Tzedek (C) *4099 Pine Island Road 741-0295*
Chabad Lubavitch (O) *4561 North University Drive 748-1777*
Temple Bet Tikvah (R) *8890 West Oakland Park Boulevard 741-8088*
Surfside Congregation Mogen David (O) *9348 Harding Avenue (305) 865-9714*
Tallahassee 32303 Temple Israel (R) *2215 Mahan Drive (904) 877-3517*
Congregation Shomrai Torah (C) *1115 North Gadsen Street 222-1667*
Tamarac Temple Beth Torah (C) *9101 N.W. 57th Street (305) 721-7660*
Congregation Migdal David (O) *8575 West McNab Road 726-3583*
North Lauderdale Hebrew Congregation (C) *6050 Baily Road 727-7383*
Congregation Beth Tefilah (C) *6435 West Commercial Boulevard 722-7607*
Tampa 33609 Chabad Lubavitch (O) *3620 Fletcher Avenue (813) 971-6768*
Temple David (T) *2001 Swaan Avenue 251-4215*
Congregation Kol Ami (C) *3919 Moran Road 962-6338*
Rodeph Sholom Congregation (C) *2713 Bayshore Boulevard 837-1911*

Congregation Schaarai Zedek (R)   3303 *Swaan Avenue*
876-2377

Vero Beach   Temple Beth Sholom (R)   365 *43rd Avenue*
(305) 569-4700

Wellington   Temple Beth Torah (R)   793-2700

West Palm Beach   33407   Congregation Aitz Chaim (O)
North Haberhill Road
(305) 686-5055
Congregation Anshei Sholom (C)   5348 *Grove Street*
684-3212
Temple Beth El (C)   2815 *North Flagler Drive*   833-0339
Temple B'nai Jacob (C)   2177 *South Congress Street*   433-5957
Golden Lakes Temple (C)   1470 *Golgen Lakes Boulevard*
689-9430
Temple Israel (R)   1901 *North Flagler Drive*   833-8421
Temple Judea (R)   4000 *Washington Road*   471-1526

THE OLD NEIGHBORHOODS

The following list contains information about synagogues which are no longer functioning as Jewish houses of worship. These addresses are located in the old sections of the city or town. It is advisable to take extra precautions while driving through these neighborhoods.

Belle Glade   Beth Torah Congregation   *200 East Palm Street*
Temple Beth Sholom   *N.W. Avenue G*
Clearwater   Congregath Beth Sholom   *2177 Coachman Avenue, N.E.*
Congregations Sons of Jacob   *1230 Brookside Drive*
Cocoa Beach   Temple Israel   *15 Poinsetta Drive*
Coral Gables   First Hebrew Congregation   *2410 Ponce de Leon Boulevard*
Temple Shira   *3511 Riviera Drive*
Coral Gables Jewish Center   *320 Palermo Avenue*
Daytona Beach   Temple Beth El   *507 5th Street*
Fort Lauderdale   Temple Emanu-El   *1801 South Andrews Avenue*
Tamarac Jewish Center   *9106 N.W. 57th Street*
Fort Pierce   Temple Beth El   *302 North 23rd Street*
Gainesville   Temple B'nai Israel   *333 West Masonic Street*
3115 N.W. 16th Street
Hialeah   Hialeah Reform Temple   *595 West 68th Street*
Temple Israel   *South Tropical Trail*
Hollywood   Temple Beth Ahm   *310 S.W. 62nd Avenue*
Temple Beth Sholom   *4601 Arthur Street*
1725 Monroe Street
Young Israel   *3550 North 54th Avenue*

Jacksonville Temple Ahavath Chesed   *1708 Mallory Street*
Eitz Chaim Synagogue   *29 West 6th Street*
Jacksonville Jewish Center   *10101 San Jose Boulevard*
  205 West 3rd Street

Key West B'nai Zion Congregation   *19th & Delancey Streets*

Miami Congregation Anshei Emes   *2533 S.W. 19th Avenue*
  Israelite Center Temple   *3175 S.W. 25th Street*
  Israel South Temple   *9025 Sunset Drive*
  Temple Beth David   *Avenue H & 10th Street*
  Temple Israel   *S.W. 12th Avenue & 4th Street*
  Temple Or Olam   *8755 S.W. 16th Street*
  Temple Tifereth Israel   *6500 North Miami Avenue*

Miami Beach Cuban Sephardic Hebrew Congregation
  1200 Normandy Drive
  Congregation Etz Chaim   *1544 Washington Avenue*
  Sky Lake Synagogue   *18151 N.E. 19th Avenue*

Ocala *United Hebrew Congregation*   North 2nd Street

Orlando Congregation of Liberal Judaism   *301 Ferncreek Street*
  Congregation Ohev Sholom   *602 East Church Street*

Pembroke Pines Temple in the Pines   *1900 University Drive*

Pensacola Temple Beth El   *Chase Street*
Congregation B'nai Israel   *400 North Barcelona Street*

Plantation Plantation Jewish Congregation   *400 South Nob Hill Road*

St. Petersburg Temple Beth El   *757 Arlington Avenue, North*
  Congregation B'nai Israel   *1039 Arlington Avenue, North*
  Temple Hillel   *8195 38th Street*

Sanford Congregation Beth Am

Sarasota Temple Beth Sholom   *Washington Boulevard & 12th Street*

Tallahassee   Temple Israel   *503 South Copeland Street*
   1110 Laswade Drive

Tampa   Rodeph Sholom Congregation   *309 East Palm Avenue*
Congregation Beth Israel   *2111 Swaan Avenue*
Congregation Schaarai Zedek   *508 South Delaware Street*
Congregation Kneses Israel   *Oak & Central Street*

West Palm Beach   Temple Beth El   *630 Fern Street*

GEORGIA

Georgia was founded in 1732 by James Oglethorpe, a member of Parliament, who sought a place where imprisoned English debtors might start a free and new life. Forty-two Jews landed in Savannah on July 11, 1733. This was the largest group of Jews ever to land in North America in Colonial days. They were all Sephardic Jews, except for two families, Benjamin Sheftall's and Abraham Minis', who stemmed from Ashkenazic backgrounds.

In July, 1735, the first synagogue in Georgia, Kahal Kodesh Mickva Israel, was organized. In 1742, the Spanish fleet threatened to invade Savannah. The Sephardic Jews fled to Charleston, South Carolina, since in the Catholic Church's eyes, these former *Marranos* were guilty of the crime of apostasy.

By 1786, the Jews returned and reorganized the congregation. On July 21, 1820, the first synagogue to be erected in the State of Georgia, was consecrated. That small wooden structure, located on the northwest corner of Liberty and Whitaker Streets, was destroyed by fire on December 4, 1829, though the Torahs and the Ark were saved without injury. Efforts to rebuild were begun in 1834 and a new brick building on the same site was consecrated by Reverend Isaac Leeser, of Philadelphia, in 1841.

The Reform Movement was well underway in America by the middle of the 19th century. The congregation favored the Portuguese *minhag* (ritual) but slowly introduced changes in the ritual in 1868 by omitting the celebration of the second day of festivals and by introducing a choir with music. Later, marriage canopies were made optional and then members were permitted to go hatless during services. The Portuguese *minhag* remained in use until 1895, when Mickve Israel printed its own prayer books. In 1902, the Union Prayer Book was adopted, and on January 10, 1904, Mickve Israel joined the Union of American Hebrew Congregations.

By 1874, it had become apparent that the small synagogue built on Liberty Street and Perry Lane was no longer adequate for the congregation. On March 1, 1876, the cornerstone was laid for the present building and the Monterey Square Temple was consecrated on April 11, 1878. It was designed by a church architect in perfect 14th century Gothic style.

Other Jewish communities in Georgia, before the Civil War were located in Augusta (1825), Atlanta (1845), Macon (1850), and Columbus (1854). The best known Jewish Georgian before the Civil War was Rapheal J. Moses. He was an ardent secessionist and opposed any compromise with the North. He assisted General Robert E. Lee in relieving the food shortages in the state during the war. As Confederate Commissary of Georgia, Moses held gold bullion boxes set aside for the benefit of returning soldiers.

The first Jews arrived in Atlanta when it was still called Marthasville in the 1840s. One of the first Jewish families in Atlanta, the Rich's, started a small clothing store in 1867. It became Rich's Department Store, one of the largest merchandising enterprises in the South. Most of the data about the history of the Jewish community of Atlanta before the Civil War was destroyed when General Sherman's armies burned the city.

The oldest congregation in Atlanta, the Hebrew Benevolent Congregation, was dedicated in 1877 and has been known as The Temple. In 1895, The Temple joined the Reform Movement. Its rabbi for fifty years was Rabbi David Marx. A member of The Temple was Leo Frank. In 1913, Leo Frank was accused of murdering a 14-year old employee in his pencil factory, Mary Phagan. The jury found him guilty as charged, although there was very little evidence against him. This was a classic case of blood libel.

His case was appealed to the United States Supreme Court. He was to be sentenced to be hanged but because of the public outcry from outside Jewish and non-Jewish communities, his sentence was commuted ro life imprisonment. This infuriated many anti-Semitic Georgians. On the night of August 16, 1915, a mob stormed into the State Prison Farm and carried Leo Frank to Marietta, 125 miles away, where Mary Phagan was buried, and lynched him from a tree. Years later, Leo Frank was exonerated of the crime which has been committed by an employee of his. Rabbi Marx was threatened since he defended Frank. After the lynching, Rabbi Marx was smuggled aboard the train that carried Frank's body to New York for burial.

Following the incident, Jewish businessmen throughout the state were threatened by the Knights of Mary Phagan. It was during this period that the Knights of the Ku Klux Klan was organized at Stone Mountain, outside Atlanta.

Rabbi Jacob Rothschild succeeded Rabbi Marx at The Temple. He was an exponent of racial equality. It was because of his active role in the Civil Rights movement that on October 12, 1958, The Temple was bombed by 50 sticks of dynamite. President Eishenhower denounced this attack on The Temple. Atlantans of all faiths contributed toward its rebuilding.

There are approximately 30,700 Jews living in Georgia, of which about 22,000 reside in Atlanta.

ATLANTA

THE TEMPLE
1589 Peachtree Road, N.W.

Organized as the Hebrew Benevolent Society in 1877, The Temple is the oldest congregation in Atlanta. It has followed the Reform ritual since 1895. The Temple is a brick structure trimmed with limestone of Nineteenth Century Georgian architecture. The main auditorium seats 750 people with 150 additional seats located in the balcony. A unique feature in The Temple is the Ark which rises from the floor during services. The religious school adjoins the main building and contains 16 classrooms and an auditorium seating 450 people. The architects were Hentz, Adler & Shutze.

In 1958, The Temple was fire-bombed by the Ku Klux Klan because of the active role in the Civil Rights movement of its then rabbi, Jacob Rothschild. Citizens in Atlanta of all faiths contributed toward its rebuilding.

ATHENS

CONGREGATION CHILDREN OF ISRAEL
Dudley Drive

Organized in 1872, Kol Kadush Beni Yisroile, built its first house of worship on the corner of Hancock and Jackson Streets in 1884. It remained at that location until 1968, when its new and present structure was dedicated. The move was initiated because of the

The Temple is Atlanta's oldest congregation.

expansion at the University of Georgia and government research facilities opening the way for a large number of new faculty members. Among these were several Jews coming to live in the South for the first time.

UNIVERSITY OF GEORGIA

Located adjoining the former synagogue building of Congregation Children of Israel, at Jackson and Hancock Streets, is the Stern Community House. It was built by Mrs. Myer Stern as a memorial to her husband. This area housed several of the leading Jewish citizens of Athens.

The Athens Regional Library, at College and Hancock Streets, was originally built as the mansion of Charles Stern. The Micheal brothers built twin mansions on Prince Avenue at Grady Street. These showplaces which were connected by a *porte cochere*, were between the Grady House and the house presently occupied by the President of the University of Georgia. The B'nai B'rith Hillel Foundation occupies the house on Milledge Avenue which once belonged to Sol and Minnie Boley.

COLUMBUS

TEMPLE ISRAEL
1617 Wildwood Avenue

In 1854, a group of twenty Jewish families from Germany banded together to found Temple B'nai Israel. The first synagogue was located at 318 10th Street and was dedicated in 1887. In 1907, a tragic fire destroyed the interior. It was rebuilt and remodelled but remained in its Downtown location until 1958. In March of 1958, the congregation dedicated its present synagogue on Wildwood Avenue.

The first President of the congregation, Moses Myers, came from Filehne, Germany. He avoided conscription into the Confederate Army during the Civil War with an injury to his leg which required that he hobble about on crutches through the war years, but which became "miraculously cured" at war's end.

*Congregation Children of Israel's first building at Hancock &
Jackson Streets.*

SAVANNAH

CONGREGATION MICKVE ISRAEL
20 Gordon Street

The oldest synagogue in Georgia, Congregation Mickve Israel, was founded in July, 1733, five months after the establishment of the colony of Georiga. The first synagogue in the state, and the third oldest in the United States, was built in 1820 on the northwest corner of Liberty and Whitaker Streets. The event has been commemorated by a bronze plaque embedded in the sidewalk.

The small wooden structure was destroyed by fire on December 4, 1829, though the Torahs and the Ark were saved without injury. Efforts to rebuild were begun in 1834 and a new brick building on the same site was consecrated by Reverend Isaac Leeser of Philadelphia, in 1841.

Savannah participated in the great wave of German Jewish immigration that began in the 1840s. By 1874, it had become apparent that the small synagogue on Liberty Street and Perry Lane was no longer adequate for the growing congregation. On March 1, 1876, the cornerstone was laid for the present building and the Monterey Square Temple was consecrated on April 11, 1878.

The synagogue was designed in pure 14th century Gothic by the English architect, Henry G. Harrison. The synagogue houses a Jewish museum containing a 1733 Torah; seven Presidential letters, including Washington's, Jefferson's, and Madison's; and a 1790 Minute Book. For information about the synagogue and the Jewish museum call (912) 233-1547.

Savannah River

Cap'n. Sam River Cruises

W. RIVER ST. E. RIVER ST.
FACTORS WALK
City Hall
Emmet Ships of the Sea Maritime Museum Park ST.
W. BAY ST. E. BAY

U.S. Customs
Cotton & Naval Stores Exchange

W. BRYAN ST. E. BRYAN ST.
William Scarborough House | Franklin Square | Ellis Square | Johnson Square | Reynolds Square | Warren Square | Washington Square

W. CONGRESS ST. E. CONGRESS ST.
W. BROUGHTON ST. Christ Episcopal Church E. BROUGHTON ST.

ZULBY ST.
STATE | Telfair Mansion & Art Museum | Federal ST. Bldg. | Evangelical Lutheran Church | Owens-Thomas House & Museum | Davenport House | Museum of Antique Dolls
E. STATE

Court House | PRES-IDENT | Telfair Square | Wright Square Post Office | Oglethorpe Square | Columbia Square PRES-IDENT | Greene Square ST.

W. YORK ST.
YORK ST.
Complex | W. OGLETHORPE AVE. | E. OGLETHORPE AVE. HOUSTON

Greyhound Terminal | Trailways Terminal | CIVIC | Independent Presbyterian Church | J.G. Low Birthplace | Fire Dept. | HULL | Police
W. HULL ST. E.

Elbert Square | Municipal Auditorium | Orleans Square | Chippewa Square | Colonial Park Cemetery | Crawford Square
The Great Savannah Exposition | CENTER | PERRY | PERRY LA.
Chamber of Commerce | W. LIBERTY ST. E. LIBERTY ST.

LOUIS-VILLE RD.
Visitors Center | JEFFERSON | BARNARD | WHITAKER | DRAYTON | ABERCORN | LINCOLN | HABERSHAM | PRICE | EAST | BROAD

W. HARRIS ST. E. HARRIS ST.
Pulaski Square | Green-Meldrim Home | Madison Square | Colonial Dames House | Lafayette Square | Cathedral of St. John the Baptist | Troup Square

W. CHARLTON ST. E. Andrew Low Home CHARLTON ST.
W. JONES ST. E. JONES ST.

SELMA ST.
WEST | MONTGOMERY
W. TAYLOR ST. E. TAYLOR ST.
16 | Chatham Square | Monterrey Square | Temple Mikve Israel | Calhoun Square | Whitfield Square

W. GORDON ST. E. GORDON ST.

W. GASTON ST. E. GASTON ST.

Forsyth Park
To King-Tisdell Cottage

DOWNTOWN SAVANNAH

N

Mickve Israel Temple was designed in the Gothic style in 1876.

SHEFTALL HOUSE
321 East York Street

Located in the Savannah Historical Area, the Sheftall House is a frame building erected in 1810 by a member of the Sheftall family. Benjamin Sheftall was one of the first Jews to settle in Savannah in 1733. He was the only Ashkenazic Jew among the first 43 Jewish settlers. The others were Sephardim of Portuguese origin.

SHEFTALL BURIAL GROUND
Cohen and Spruce Streets

This small Jewish cemetery was dedicated in 1773 by Levi Sheftall as a family burial ground.

OLD JEWISH CEMETERY

This plot of land was donated to the Jewish community in 1773 by Mordecai Sheftall. It remained in use until 1850 and is now an official Historic Landmark.

SYNAGOGUES

Albany   31702   Albany Hebrew Congregation (R)   *200 South Jefferson Street   (912) 432-6536*

Athens   30606   Congregation Children of Israel (R) *Dudley Drive   (404) 549-4192*

Atlanta   30327   Congregation Ahavath Achim (C)   600 *Peachtree Battle Avenue, N.W.   (404) 355-5222*
Congregation Anshe Sfard (O)   *1324 North Highland Avenue, N.W.   872-9045*
Congregation Beth Jacob (O)   *1855 La Vista Road   633-0551*
Congregation Beth Sholom (C)   *3147 Chablee-Tucker Road 458-0489*
Congregation B'nai Torah (T)   *700 Mount Vernon Highway 257-0537*
Congregation Beth Tefillah (Chabad) (O)   *6600 Roswell Road Suite G   843-2464*
Congregation Or Vesholom (T)   *1681 North Druid Hills Road, N.E.   633-1737*
Congregation Shearith Israel (T)   *1180 University Drive, N.E. 873-1743*
Temple Emanu-El (R)   *1580 Spalding Drive   395-1340*
Congregation Kehilat Chaim (R)   *141 Wienca Road, N.W. (Suite 101)   252-4441*
Temple Sinai (R)   *5645 Dupree Drive, N.W.   252-3073*
The Temple (R)   *1589 Peachtree Road, N.E.   873-1731*

Augusta   30904   Congregation Adas Yeshurun (O)   935 *Johns Road   (404) 733-9491*
Congregation Children of Israel (R)   *3005 Walto Way 736-3140*

Bainbridge   31717   Temple Beth El (R)   *Broad & Evans Street   (912) 432-6536*

Brunswick   31520   Temple Beth Tefilot (R)   *1326 Egmont Street   (912) 265-7575*

Columbus   31906   Temple Israel (R)   *1617 Wildwood Avenue*   *(404) 323-1617*
Shearith Israel Synagogue (C)   *2550 Wynnton Road*   *323-1443*

Dalton   30720   Temple Beth El (C)   *501 Valley Drive*   *(404) 278-6798*

La Grange   30240   Congregation Beth El (C)   *210 Church Street*   *(404) 884-7708*

Macon   31201   Temple Beth Israel (R)   *892 Cherry Street*   *(912) 745-6727*
Congregation Shearith Israel (C)   *611 First Street*   *745-4571*

Riverdale   Congregation B'nai Israel (R)   *2165 Highway 138*   *(404) 471-3586*

Rome   30161   Rodeph Sholom Congregation (R)   *406 East 1st Street*   *(404) 291-0678*

Savannah   31401   Congregation Agudath Achim (C)   *9 Lee Boulevard*   *(912) 352-4737*
Congregation B'nai B'rith Jacob (O)   *5444 Abercorn Street*   *354-7721*
Congregation Mickve Israel (R)   *20 East Gordon Street*   *233-1547*

Snellville   Temple Beth David (R)   *869 Cole Road*   *(404) 979-2773*

Valdosta   31601   Temple Israel (C)   *511 Baytree Road*   *(912) 244-1813*

THE OLD NEIGHBORHOODS

The following list contains information about synagogues which are no longer functioning as Jewish houses of worship. These addresses are located in the old sections of the city or town. It is advisable to take extra precautions while driving through these neighborhoods.

Albany   Albany Hebrew Congregation   *Jefferson & Commerce Streets*

Athens   Congregation Children of Israel   *Jackson & Hancock Streets*

Atlanta   Congregation Ahavath Achim   *Piedmont & Gilmer Streets*
346 Washington Street, S.W.
Congregation Or Vesholom   *500 Washington Street, S.W.*
Temple of Israel   *891-Mayson Turner Avenue N.W.*

Augusta   Congregation Children of Israel   *1120 Ellis Street*

Columbus   Temple Israel   *318 10th Street*

Fitzgerald   Hebrew Congregation   *615 South Sherman Street*
Lee & Magnolia Streets

Savannah   Congregation Agudath Achim   *912 Drayton Street*
Congregation B'nai B'rith Jacob   *112 Montgomery Street*
Mickve Israel   *Liberty & Whitaker Streets*

Thomasville   Congregation B'nai Israel   *210 South Crawford Street*

Valdosta   Hebrew Congregation   *600 West Park Avenue*
Smithland Place

Vidalia   Congregation Beth Israel   *Aimwell Road*

Waycross   Hebrew Congregation   *507 Elizabeth Street*
710 Screven Avenue

West Point   Congregation Beth El

LOUISIANA

Louisiana was occupied by the French and Spanish before the territory was purchased by the Americans in 1803. Under French law, the Black Code of 1724 banned the practice of Judaism in its territory.

One of the first Jews to settle in New Orleans was Judah Touro. He was the son of Isaac Touro, the Dutch-born minister of Newport, Rhode Island. He was one of the founders of Louisiana's first synagogue, Shagari (Shaari) Hesed, in 1828. He established a counting house on Royal Street. During the Battle of New Orleans, he volunteered to run ammunition to the men in the front line; consequently, he was one of the few Americans seriously wounded.

As a very successful merchant during New Orleans' "Golden Age" before the Civil War, Touro's generosity was well known, especially toward religious communities. He gave financial aid to the Catholics, Jews, Unitarians and even bought a pew in the First Christ Church Cathedral. Some of his other philanthropic activities included the founding of Touro Infirmary, the Shakespear-Touro Home for the Aged, the first free public library in the United States, and co-builder with Amos Lawrence of Boston of the Bunker Hill Monument. His generosity continued after his death by his leaving his estate equally among Protestant, Catholic, and Jewish charities.

The first synagogue in Louisiana, Shagari Hesed, was founded by German-Jewish settlers in 1828. The second congregation, Nefuzoth Yehudah, was founded in 1846 and followed the Spanish and Portuguese ritual. When the Union Army captured New Orleans in 1862, every citizen was required to take an oath of allegiance to the United States or be transported to Confederate territory. Rabbi Jacob Gutheim of the Nefuzoth Yehudah Congregation, refused to take the oath and encouraged members of his congregation to do the same even though it meant losing homes, livelihoods, and personal belongings. He left the city in May, 1863 and spent the war years as rabbi of the congregation in Montgomery, Alabama.

After the Civil War both congregations, Shagari Hesed and Nefuzoth Yehudah, found that they could not exist independently and they consolidated in 1881 to become the Touro Synagogue, bearing the name of one of the great leaders of the New Orleans Jewish community, Judah Touro.

Other Jewish settlements were founded throughout the state including Alexandria (1854), Donaldsville (1854), Plaquemine (1856), Baton Rouge (1858), Shreveport (1848), Morgan City (1859), Monroe (1861), Bastrop (1877), Opelousas (1877), and Natchitoches (1871). The Jewish population of Louisiana is approximately 17,300.

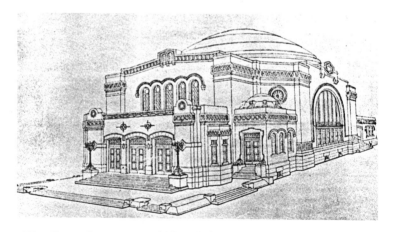

The Touro Synagogue of New Orleans — original sketch by architect Emile Weil, 1907.

NEW ORLEANS

TOURO SYNAGOGUE
4238 St. Charles Avenue

The Touro Synagogue is the home of the oldest Jewish congregation in the Mississippi Valley. It is an amalgamation of the German-Jewish settlers "Shagarai Hesed," founded in 1828, and the Spanish and Portuguese Jewish community "Nefuzoth Yehudah," founded in 1846. They consolidated in 1881 to become the Touro Synagogue, bearing the name of Judah Touro, one of the founders of the Jewish community in New Orleans.

The present-day Touro Synagogue, consecrated and dedicated in 1909, was built by the New Orleans architect, Emil Weil. Its handsome dome is typical of the Byzantine architecture adopted by many synagogues at the turn of the century. At the top of the dome is a blue stained-glass representing the Heaven of Heavens. Both the pulpit and the Holy Ark were made at the personal behest of Judah Touro, who sent to the Middle East so the pillars on either side of the Ark could be made of authentic Cedars of Lebanon, like the Holy Temple built by Solomon in Jerusalem. The congregation follows the Reform ritual.

DISPERSED OF JUDAH (NEFUZOTH YEHUDAH) CEMETERY
North Side of Upper Canal Street (near City Park Avenue)

Judah Touro, one of the founders of the Jewish community of New Orleans, was buried here. His remains were later sent to Newport, Rhode Island for reburial. There is an historic inscription commemorating this event.

The First Jewish Cemetery, oldest in Louisiana, located at Jackson Avenue and Saratoga Street, dates from the 1820s. It is still intact but has not been used since the end of the Civil War.

TEMPLE SINAI
6227 St. Charles Avenue

In 1870, in response to the Reform Movement sweeping the Jewish communities throughout the entire United States, Temple Sinai was organized, the first Reform congregation in New Orleans. Within two years, the first Temple Sinai was completed near Lee Circle, but by the early 1920s a new temple was needed. The present site on St. Charles Avenue was chosen and in 1928 the new temple was dedicated.

In 1949, when Dr. Ralph Bunche, former United Nations mediator for Palestine, came to New Orleans to speak, he could find no auditorium available for an unsegregated audience. Rabbi Julian Feibleman opened Temple Sinai's auditorium to an overflowing meeting sponsored by the Inter-Racial Committee of New Orleans and an historic precedent was set. In 1858, Rabbi Feibleman was the first rabbi to have been present at the coronation of a pope.

LAKE CHARLES

TEMPLE SINAI
713 Hodges Street

The Temple Sinai is of distinctive Byzantine design with twelve elaborate matched windows of English stained-glass. Two metal spires, destroyed in the 1918 hurricane, were never replaced. The congregation follows the Reform ritual.

Temple Sinai of Lake Charles, Louisiana.

SYNAGOGUES

Alexandria   71301   Congregation B'nai Israel (C)   *1907
Vance Street   (318) 445-4586*
Congregation Gemilas Chassodim (R)   *2021 Turner Street*
445-3655

Baton Rouge   70806   Congregation B'nai Israel (R)   *3354
Kleinert Avenue   (504) 343-0111*
Liberal Synagogue (R)   *9111 Jefferson Highway   924-6773*

Lafayette   70501   Temple Rodeph Sholom (R)   *603 Lee
Street   (318) 234-3760*
Yeshurun Synagogue (R)   *1520 Kaliste Saloom Road
984-1775*

Lake Charles   70601   Temple Sinai (R)   *713 Hodges Street
(318) 439-2866*

Metairie   70002   Congregation Gates of Prayer (R)
4000 West Esplanade Avenue   (504) 885-2600
Tikvat Sholom Congregation (C)   *3737 West Esplanade Avenue
889-1144*
Young Israel (O)   *4428 Courtland Drive   887-6997*

Monroe   71201   Congregation B'nai Israel (R)   *2400 Orell
Place (318) 387-0730*

Morgan City   70380   Temple Shaare Zedek (R)   *315 3rd
Street*

New Orleans   70124   Congregation Anshe Sfard (O)
2230 Carondelet Street   (504) 522-4714
Beth Israel Congregation (O)   *7000 Canal Boulevard
283-4366*
Chabad Lubavitch (O)   *7037 Freret Street   866-5164*
Congregation Chevre Tehillim (O)   *4429 South Clairbourne
Avenue   895-7987*
Temple Sinai (R)   *6227 St. Charles Avenue   861-3693*
Touro Synagogue (R)   *4238 St. Charles Avenue   895-4843*

Shreveport   71105   Congregation Agudath Achim (C)
9401 *Village Green Drive*   *(318) 797-6401*
B'nai Zion Congregation (R)   *175 Southfield Road*   *861-2122*

THE OLD NEIGHBORHOODS

The following list contains information about synagogues which are no longer functioning as Jewish houses of worship. These addresses are located in the old sections of the city or town. It is advisable to take extra precautions while driving through these neighborhoods.

Alexandria   Congregation B'nai Israel   *2007 Thornton Street*
Congregation Gemilath Chassodim   *4th & Fisk Streets*
Baton Rouge   Congregation B'nai Israel   *Laurel & 5th Streets*
Liberal Synagogue   *Oakwood & Wilshire Drives*
260 South Acadia Thruway
Basrop   B'nai Sholom Congregation
Bogalusa   Congregation Beth El
Lafayette   Temple Rodeph Sholom   *438 Jefferson Street*
Monroe   Congregation B'nai Israel   *400 Jackson Street*
Morgan City   Temple Shaare Zedek   *708 3rd Street*
Natchitoches   Congregation B'nai Israel   *2nd Street*
New Iberia   Congregation Gates of Prayer   *Charles & Weeks Streets*
New Orleans   Beth Israel Congregation   *1629 Euterpe Street*

Congregation Gates of Prayer   *Napoleon & Colosseum Streets*
Jackson Avenue, between Annunciation & Chippewa Streets
Conservative Congregation   *932 Napoleon Avenue*
Temple Sinai   *Lee Circle*
Westbank Congregation   *3701 Behrman Place*

Opelousas   Temple Emanu-El   *747 South Main Street*
541 South Main Street

Shreveport   Congregation Agudath Achim   *1707 Line*
Avenue
B'nai Zion Congregation   *802 Cotton Street*
Fannin Street

Plaquemine   Congregation Ohavai Sholom

MISSISSIPPI

The Fort of Natchez, or Rosalie as it was called originally, was founded by the French in 1714. It was in the midst of lush country, high above the Mississippi River. Its founders were patriotic Frenchmen, devoted servants of the French king, and zealous for the Catholic faith. In 1722, they issued a law, "Compelling owners to bring up their slaves in the faith of the Catholics, or if the owners were not good Catholics themselves, their slaves should be owned by the government... Jews were to be expelled and no other religion was to be tolerated." These laws were incorporated in the *Black Code*. It was called the Black Code because it dealt chiefly with Negro slaves. It was a simple matter to bar Jews from the village which was small, but it was hard to keep them out of the territory which was vast.

The earliest known names of Jewish residents in Natchez are those of Benjamin Monsanto and his wife, Clara. They lived during the Spanish rule and were not clandestine as Marranos or "secret Jews," but were known as Jews. A General Ezekiel Forman visited Natchez shortly after the American Revolutionary War. He recorded in his journal that he had met a charming Spanish-Jewish couple whose hospitality he had enjoyed. Benjamin Monsanto had a plantation on St. Catherine's Creek and dealt in slaves, farm animals, and real estate. Most of the early Jewish arrivals, however, were Germans from Alsace Lorraine and became peddlers and branched out into the country as storekeepers and cotton brokers.

Natchez has the oldest Jewish community in continuous existence. The oldest existing congregation in Mississippi is B'nai Israel. It was established in 1845. It was organized as an Orthodox congregation. On September 3, 1865, before the High Holy Day, seven rules were drawn up for the worshippers' guidance during Divine Services:

1. Members on entering the House of Worship will take their proper seats. Strangers will have their seats assigned to them by the Warden.
2. It is expected that persons will be orderly and quiet during Divine Services.
3. No person will leave the synagogue during the reading of the Torah.
4. The congregation will rise and continue standing during the recitation of certain portions, the presiding officers giving the example.
5. Members and others are kindly requested to conduct their devotions in such a manner so as not to interfere with the Reader.
6. Persons are not allowed to change seats or walk about the room during services.
7. Children under five years of age, will not be permitted to be brought to the synagogue.

The ritual, order of services, was European; the *Minhag America*, the modified American order, was rejected until 1871. Temple B'nai Israel was one of the founding members of the Union of American Hebrew Congregations in 1873. The congregation built its first synagogue on the corner of Washington and Commerce Streets in 1872. The cornerstone was laid by Dr. Isaac Mayer Wise. The dedicatory address was delivered by Dr. Max Lilienthal. On Saturday afternoon, November 21, 1903, the temple burned down. The Jefferson Street Methodist Church offered the free use of its building. On March 24, 1905, the present temple building on Washington Street was dedicated.

On December 17, 1862, General Ulyses S. Grant issued the notorious Order No. 11 from Holly Springs, Mississippi. It expelled all Jews as a class from the Department of Tennessee, which included Mississippi. This decree was issued because of the general anarchy, chaos, bribery, and corruption that was responsible for the widespread profiteering by Northerners in Southern cotton.

The Jews were blamed for this state of anarchy. The Order No. 11 was quickly repealed by President Abraham Lincoln.

The breakdown of the plantation system after the Civil War transferred the status and economic power from the farms to the cities. The store now brought about the growth of the cities. One effect of this development was a postwar influx of Jewish merchants and storekeepers. The Jews in postwar Mississippi became an important factor in the economic rebuilding of the state. They became rural businessmen, mill operators, cotton brokers, and professional men.

Other early Jewish communities in the state include Vicksburg (1846), Port Gibson (1858), Jackson (1858), and Meridian (1869). The Jewish population of Mississippi is approximately 4,000.

JACKSON

BETH ISRAEL CONGREGATION
5315 Old Cotton Road

The congregation built the first synagogue in the state in 1861. It was destroyed during the Civil War when most of Jackson was sacked. The second synagogue, built in 1867, was destroyed by fire. The congregation's third building was built in 1874 on the corner of South State Street and East South Street. That building was sold in 1940. In 1942, the congregation built a temple on Woodrow Wilson Avenue across from Millsaps College campus. During World War II, the building was used as a weekend entertainment and comfort center for the servicemen in the area. In 1967, the present temple on the Old Cotton Road was dedicated. On September 18, 1967, the new temple was bombed; on November 21, 1967, the rabbi's home was bombed. The rabbi, Perry

Nussbaum, was a strong advocate of civil rights for blacks. In 1985, the congregation celebrated its 125th anniversary.

Beth Israel of Jackson, Mississippi was organized in 1861.

NATCHEZ

TEMPLE B'NAI ISRAEL
606 Washington Street

Founded in 1845 as the Congregation Chevra Kadischa B'nai Israel as an Orthodox congregation. It is the oldest Jewish congregation in Mississippi. In 1873, it was one of the founding members of the Union of American Hebrew Congregations—the Reform Movement. The congregation's first building of 1872 was destroyed by fire. The present building was dedicated in 1905. Due to the recent decline in the Jewish population in Natchez, the congregation does not have a full-time rabbi. Services are conducted, however, by student rabbis who visit the congregation once a month from the Hebrew Union College in Cincinnati, Ohio.

PORT GIBSON

TEMPLE GEMILUTH CHESSED
Church Street

The choice of an appropriate style has always been a major problem in the design of a synagogue. The architects of Temple Gemiluth Chessed succeeded in combining various Moorish, Byzantine, and Romanesque elements to produce a building unique in Mississippi. The builder, J.F. Barnes, was from Gainesville, Mississippi. The architects, Bartlett and Budemeyer, are thought to have been from St. Louis.

The horseshoe-arched entry leads to a small corridor flanked by a classroom on the left and the rabbi's study on the right. The corridor opens into the Sanctuary, which has the Ark under an elaborate horseshoe arch as its focal point. Mrs. Isador Newman, a native of Port Gibson, donated the unusal chandeliers and the Torah regalia when the temple was under construction.

When the building was dedicated on January 4, 1892, the congregation included about thirty families. Today, however, there are only four families, and services are therefore held infrequently. The congregation still maintains the old Jewish cemetery which dates back to the 1840s.

Temple Gemiluth Chassed in Port Gibson, Mississippi.

SYNAGOGUES

[Note: All area codes 601]

Biloxi   39530   Congregation Beth Israel (C)   *Camelia &
Southern Avenues*   388-5574

Clarksdale   38614   Congregation Beth Israel (R)
401 Catalpa Street   624-5862

Cleveland   38732   Temple Adath Israel (R)   *201 South
Bolivar Avenue*   843-2005

Greenville   38701   Hebrew Union Congregation (R)
504 Main Street   332-4153

Greenwood   38930   Congregation Ahavath Rayim (O)
Market Street   453-7537

Hattiesburg   39401   Congregation B'nai Israel (R)
901 Mamie Street   545-3871

Jackson   39211   Congregation Beth Israel (R)   *5315 Old
Cotton Road*   956-6215

Meridian   39302   Congregation Beth Israel (R)   *3641 46th
Street*   483-3193

Natchez   39120   Congregation B'nai Israel (R)   *213 South
Commerce Street*   445-5407

Oxford   Temple Beth Sholom (C)   *Route 1*   236-1727

Port Gibson   39150   Temple Gemilas Chassodim (R)
Church Street

Tupelo   38801   Temple B'nai Israel (C)   *Marshall & Hamlin
Streets*   842-9169

Vicksburg   39180   Temple Anshe Chesed   *2414 Grove Street*

THE OLD NEIGHBORHOODS

The following list contains information about synagogues which are no longer functioning as Jewish houses of worship. These addresses are located in the old sections of the city or town. It is advisable to take extra precautions while driving through these neighborhoods.

Brookhaven Tempel B'nai Sholom *Chickasaw & South Church Streets*

Canton B'nai Israel Congregation *Academy & Liberty Streets*

Clarksdale Congregation Beth Israel *69 Delta Street*
1124 Rose Circle Drive

Columbus Congregation B'nai Israel *717 2nd Avenue, North*

Greenwood Temple Beth Israel *400 East Adams Street*
Williamson & Washington Streets

Jackson Congregation Beth Israel *South State Street & East South Street*
Woodrow Wilson Drive

Laurel Knesseth Israel Congregation *802 5th Avenue*

Lexington Temple Beth El *224 Court Square*
Spring Street

Meridian Congregation Beth Israel *5718 14th Place*
11th Street & 24th Avenue
8th Street & 22nd Avenue

Natchez Congregation B'nai Israel *606 Washington Street*

Port Gibson Temple Gemilas Chassodim *Cotton Street*

Vicksburg Temple Anshe Chesed *1209 Cherry Street*

NORTH CAROLINA

The earliest Jews to settle in North Carolina came from Barbados and were of Spanish-Portuguese origin. Although North Carolina was among the first of the 13 colonies to welcome Jewish settlements, the first settlement of any significance did not develop until the middle of the 19th century. Jewish peddlers who had immigrated from Germany started small Jewish communities in Wilmington, Albertville, and Yanceyville. These locations were "way stations" for the peddlers. They returned on Friday in time to observe the Sabbath. These peddlers dealt with the Cherokee Indians, who dubbed them "egg-eaters" since the peddlers avoided any meat while they were on the road.

Fifty-two Jews from North Carolina fought with the Confederate Army during the Civil War, including six brothers from the Cohen family. The first Jew to die for the Confederacy was Albert Lurie Moses of Charlotte, who died heroically at the Battle of Seven Pines. Abe Weil of Charlotte gave refuge in his home to Jefferson P. Davis, President of the Confederate States of America, when Union forces were hunting him.

Many Jewish peddlers became store owners and merchants and a considerable number acquired great wealth and distinction such as Joseph Fels, founder of Fels Naptha Company. The Cone family of Greensboro built one of the South's greatest textile complexes. They were the first in the cotton industry to organize world distribution, and were also pioneers in the establishment of a comprehensive welfare program for their employees.

North Carolina's first congregation was established in Wilmington in 1867 and formally incorporated as Temple of Israel in 1873. Other congregations were organized in New Bern (1881),

Goldsboro (1878), Greensboro (1880), Tarboro (1874), Durham (1880), Raleigh (1879), and Winston-Salem (1890).

BEAUFORT

JACOB HENRY HOUSE
229 Front Street

Jacob Henry was elected to the State Legislature in 1808. He was asked to take an oath of office on the New Testament otherwise he would be expelled from office. Jacob Henry delivered an eloquent speech in defense of full religious liberty for all. He was ultimately permitted to keep his seat in the State Legislature on a technicality. The two-story frame dwelling built between 1794-1802 is a National Historic Landmark.

CHARLOTTE

JUDAH P. BENJAMIN MEMORIAL
Sidewalk Marker on South Tyron Street

This memorial was erected in 1948 by Temple Beth El and Temple Israel of Charlotte. It commemorates Judah P. Benjamin, Confederate Secretary of State and Secretary of War, who found refuge in Charlotte in the last days of the Civil War. The marker is on the site of the home of Abraham Weil, a Jewish merchant, who played host to Benjamin while Union forces were hunting him.

Judah P. Benjamin, pictured on the Confederate two-dollar bill, was the Secretary of State and Secretary of War of the Confederacy.

HEBREW CEMETERY
McCall Street at Oaklawn Avenue

The remains of prominent Jewish families are buried in this cemetery including Aaron Cohen and a number of Confederate soldiers.

GOLDSBORO

TEMPLE OHEB SHOLOM
314 North James Street

Organized in 1883, the small Romanesque Revival brick building was built by Milton Harding. The building is slated to become a National Historic Landmark.

SOLOMON WEIL HOUSE and HENRY WEIL HOUSE
200 and 204 West Chestnut Street

One of the first Jewish settlers in Goldsboro was Henry Weil. After serving in the Confederate Army, he opened H. Weil & Bros., a small general store that grew into one of North Carolina's leading department stores. Members of the Weil family were among the founders of Congregation Oheb Sholom in 1883.

These two homes were designed in 1875 by G.S.H. Appleget. The twin frame Italianate houses were threatened in the late 1970s and early 1980s with demolition for a County Office Building parking lot. They were saved and restored after a long struggle by a coalition of local preservationists working with the Historic Preservation Foundation of North Carolina. The buildings have recently been declared National Historic Landmarks.

NEW BERN

TEMPLE B'NAI SHOLOM
505 Middle Street

This Neo-Classical Revival synagogue was built in 1907. The congregation was organized in 1894. It is located within the New Bern National Register Historic District. The Jewish cemetery, located at 1707 National Avenue, was established in 1880.

STATESVILLE

CONGREGATION EMANU-EL
206 Kelly Street

Congregation Emanu-El was organized in 1883. The handsome brick Romanesque/Gothic Revival structure was built in 1891. It is the second oldest synagogue in North Carolina. The synagogue was closed for over 30 years as the Jewish community dwindled. It was reopened in 1956 when the state's first "circuit-riding" rabbi began his rounds. A Jewish lay leader would be entrusted with visiting scattered communities unable to maintain a synagogue or rabbi of their own. The synagogue has been declared a National Historic Landmark.

WILMINGTON

TEMPLE OF ISRAEL
1 South 4th Street

Organized in 1867, Temple of Israel dedicated the oldest synagogue in North Carolina in 1876. It was designed by Alexander Strausz in the Moorish Revival style. It has been designated a National Historic Landmark.

The B'nai Israel cemetery, established in 1898, is located at North 18th Street at Princess Place Drive.

SYNAGOGUES

Asheville   28801   Congregation Beth Ha'Tephila (R)
43 North Liberty Street   (704) 253-4911
Congregation Beth Israel (C)   229 Murdoch Avenue
252-8431

Charlotte   28207   Temple Beth El (R)   1727 Providence
Road   (704) 366-1948
Temple Beth Sholom (R)   8600 Fairview Road   366-5560
Temple Israel (C)   1014 Dilworth Road   376-2796
Lubavitch (O)   6500 Newhall Road   366-3984

Durham   27712   Beth El Congregation (C) & (O)   1004 Watt
Street   (919) 682-1238
Judea Reform Congregation (R)   2115 Cornwallis Road
489-7062

Fayetteville   28303   Congregation Beth Israel (C)
2204 Morganton Road   (919) 484-6462

Gastonia   28052   Temple Emanu-El (R)   320 South Street
(704) 865-1541

Goldsboro   Temple Oheb Sholom   314 North James Street
(919) 734-3715

Greensboro   27401   Beth David Synagogue (C)
804 Windview Drive   (919) 294-0006
Temple Emanu-El (R)   713 North Greene Street   275-6316

Hendersonville   28739   Congregation Agudas Achim (C)
328 King Street   (704) 693-9838

High Point   27260   B'nai Israel Synagogue (C)
1207 Kensington Drive   (919) 884-5522

Kingston   28501   Temple Israel (R)   Vernon & Laroque
Streets   (919) 523-2057

Raleigh   27602   Temple Beth Or (R)   5315 Creedmoor Road
(919) 781-4895

Shaarei Israel Congregation (O)   *7400 Falls of the Neuse Road*
847-8986

Statesville   28677   Congregation Emanu-El (C)
Kelly Street & West End Avenue   *(704) 873-7611*

Wilmington   28401   B'nai Israel Synagogue (C)
2601 Chestnut Street   *(919) 762-1117*
Temple of Israel (R)   *4th & Market Streets*   *762-0000*

Winston-Salem   27103   Beth Jacob Congregation (C)
1833 Academy Street   *(919) 725-3880*
Temple Emanu-El (R)   *201 Oakwood Drive*   *722-6640*

THE OLD NEIGHBORHOODS

The following list contains information about synagogues which
are no longer functioning as Jewish houses of worship. These
addresses are located in the old sections of the city or town. It is
advisable to take extra precautions while driving through these
neighborhoods.

Asheville   Congregation Beth Israel   *121 South Liberty
Street*

Chapel Hill   Judea Reform Congregation   *203 West Markham
Avenue*

Charlotte   Temple Beth Sholom   *1931 Selwyn Avenue*
United Hebrew Brotherhood   *7th Street, between Pine &
Graham Streets*

Durham   Beth El Congregation   *Halloway & Queen Streets*
Hebrew Congregation   *Main Street*

Fayetteville   Congregation Beth Israel   *1326 Fort Bragg Road*
Congregation Beth El   *Cool Spring Street*

Goldsboro   Temple Oheb Sholom   *James & Oak Streets*

Greensboro   Beth David Synagogue   *610 East Lake Street*

Hendersonville   Congregation Agudas Achim   *415 Blythe Street*

Hickory   Hickory Jewish Center   *4th Street Drive & 11th Avenue, N.W.*

High Point   B'nai Israel Synagogue   *217 Woodrow Avenue*

Jacksonville   Hebrew Congregation   *Wardola Drive*

Kingston   Congregation Tifereth Israel   *Casswell & Independent Streets*

Lumberton   Temple Beth El   *1106 Water Street*

New Bern   Temple B'nai Sholom   *233 Middle Street*
505 Middle Street

Raleigh   Temple Beth Or   *610 Hillsboro Street*
Beth Meyer Congregation   *806 West Johnson Street*
Congregation House of Jacob   *7 South East Street*

Rocky Mount   Temple Beth El   *838 Sunset Avenue*

Salisbury   Temple Beth Israel   *Brenner & Link Avenues*

Statesville   Congregation Emanu-El   *206 Kelly Street*

Weldon   Temple Emanu-El   *8th & Sycamore Streets*

Whiteville   Congregation Beth Israel   *Frink Street*

Wilmington   B'nai Israel Synagogue   *202 North 26th Street*

Wilmington   Temple of Israel   *460 Alpine Drive*
511 Orange Street

Wilson   Congregation Beth El   *Kenan & Kincaid Avenues*

Winston-Salem   Beth Jacob Congregation   *East 4th Street*
Winston Hebrew Congregation   *North Cherry Street*

SOUTH CAROLINA

Charleston was established in 1670, and the earliest known reference to a Jew in the English settlement is a description dated 1695. Soon thereafter other Jews followed, attracted by the civil and religious liberty of South Carolina and the ample economic opportunity of the colony. These pioneers were sufficiently numerous by 1749 to organize Kahal Kadosh Beth Elohim, and fifteen years later, to establish the now historic Coming Street cemetery, the oldest Jewish burial ground in the South.

Kahal Kadosh Beth Elohim is the fourth oldest Jewish congregation in the continental United States (after New York, Newport, and Savannah). At first prayers were recited in private quarters and, from 1775, in an improvised synagogue adjacent to the modern temple grounds. In 1792, construction of the largest and most impressive synagogue in the United States was commenced. It was designed by Steedman & Horlbeck, architects. It was dedicated two years later, and the visiting General Lafayette is reported to have observed the building to be "spacious and elegant." This handsome, cupolated Georgian synagogue was destroyed in the great Charleston fire of 1838 and replaced in 1840 on the same Hasell Street site by the present imposing structure.

Among notable early congregants were Moses Lindo, who before the Revolution helped to develop the cultivation of indigo (then South Carolina's second crop), and Joseph Levy, veteran of the Cherokee War of 1760-61 and probably the first Jewish officer in America. Almost two dozen men of Beth Elohim served in the War of Independence, among them the brilliant young Francis Salvador, who, as delegate to the South Carolina provincial congresses of 1775 and 1776, was one of the first Jews to serve in an

American legislature. Killed shortly after the signing of the Declaration of Independence, Salvador was also the first Jew known to die in the Revolutionary War. He was known as the "Jewish Paul Revere" because of his impassioned efforts to arouse the colonists to rebellion.

Members of the congregation founded Charleston's Hebrew Benevolent Society in 1784, the nation's oldest Jewish charitable organization, and in 1801 established the Hebrew Orphan Society, also the country's oldest, and both still active. A Hebrew school where secular as well as religious subjects were taught functioned from the middle of the eighteenth century, and in 1838 the second oldest Jewish Sunday School in the United States was organized. The blind poetess, Penina Moise, was a famous early superintendent of the school.

Other congregants pioneered in steamship navigation, introduced illuminating gas to American cities, and numbered four of the eleven founders of the country's Surpeme Council of Scottish Rite Masonry. Both the Surgeon General and the Quartermaster General of the Confederate Army belonged to Kahal Kadosh Beth Elohim. So many Charleston Jews served in the Confederate forces during the Civil War that from 1862 until the end of the War, Beth Elohim suspended trustee meetings because it was impossible to obtain a quorum. In some families, every male member capable of bearing arms was in uniform. Of the 182 Charleston Jews who saw action, 25 were killed.

Judah P. Benjamin served as Secretary of State of the Confederate States of America. In his youth, he attended Beth Elohim's religious school. At the outbreak of the Civil War, Benjamin Mordecai gave $10,000 to South Carolina's war chest. He also organized a free market which fed hundreds of needy families whose breadwinners were at the front. He also invested most of his fortune in Confederate bonds. David Lopez, who built the present synagogue of Beth Elohim, invented a torpedo boat called the *David*, which damaged many Union warships in 1863.

Beth Elohim is acknowledged as the birthplace of Reform Judaism in the United States. In 1824, a sizable group of congregants, 47 in number, petitioned the trustees of the synagogue to change the Sephardic (Spanish & Portuguese) Orthodox liturgy. The petition, which asked abridgement of the Hebrew ritual, English translations of the prayers, and a sermon in English, was denied. The disappointed liberal members thereupon resigned from the congregation and organized the "Reformed Society of Israelites." The Society, influenced by the ideas of the Hamburg Reform Congregation, the leading modernist community in Europe, lasted only nine years, but many of its progressives joined the old congregation, and while the present temple was being built in 1840, an organ was installed. With the first service in the new temple a liberalized ritual was introduced, and aside from being the first synagogue in America to include instrumental music in worship, Beth Elohim became in 1841 the first Reform congregation in the United States. It was one of the founding synagogues of the Union of American Hebrew Congregations in 1873.

There are also Jewish communities in Columbia (1830), Camden (1880), Georgetown (1900), Sumter, Darlington, Beaufort, Aiken, Florence, and Orangeburg. The Jewish population of South Carolina is approximately 8,100.

CHARLESTON

CONGREGATION KAHAL KADOSH BETH ELOHIM
86 Hasell Street

This is the oldest congregation in South Carolina and the fourth oldest synagogue in the country. It was the starting point, in 1824, of Reform Judaism in America. The building was constructed by member David Lopez from designs by the architect C.L. Warner. The temple grounds are fronted by a graceful iron fence dating from the original 1794 synagogue building which was destroyed

The original Beth Elohim was destroyed in the great Charleston fire of 1838.

in the 1838 fire.

The synagogue's design was reminiscent of a Georgian church in both its basilican plan and tall steeple. The building proudly exhibited a number of architectural elements, including its two-tiered octagonal lantern. Although the first synagogue was destroyed by the 1838 fire, it is preserved in a drawing by Solomon Nunes Carvalho. The large marble tablet above the huge entrance doors proclaims the *Shema* in Hebrew, and in the foyer in similar position is the original foundation stone of the previous synagogue. The massive Ark, which by local tradition is kept open throughout worship services, is made of Santo Domingo mahogany. Stained-glass windows, which show Jewish symbols, date from after 1886 and are replacements of windows destroyed in the earthquake of that year.

Beth Elohim has been designated a National Historic Landmark.

Beth Elohim is the oldest Reform synagogue in the world.

OLD JEWISH ORPHANAGE
88 Broad Street

Formerly the home of the First Bank of the United States, the building dates from the American Revolution. It was used as a temporary synagogue after the fire of 1838 destroyed Beth Elohim, as relief headquarters during the yellow fever epidemic of 1858, as a Jewish school, a Jewish orphan home, and a Federal court. In 1931, it was sold and became an office building. The building has been designated an Historic Landmark.

COMING STREET CEMETERY OF
CONGREGATION BETH ELOHIM
189 Coming Street

The oldest Jewish cemetery in the South and the largest Colonial Jewish burial ground, dates from 1762. There are about 600 tombstones in the cemetery, including nine Revolutionary War veterans, five veterans of the War of 1812, and eight Confederate soldiers. The cemetery is opened only by special request. Current burials are in the Huguenin Avenue Cemetery.

BRITH SHOLOM BETH ISRAEL CONGREGATION
182 Rutledge Avenue

In 1749, Charleston's first synagogue was organized. Kahal Kadosh Beth Elohim had been founded as a strictly Orthodox congregation following the Sephardic ritual of the Spanish and Portuguese Jews. In 1840, however, the members of Beth Elohim by a narrow majority voted to install an organ in the synagogue to be used as an accompaniment to services. This step marked the beginning of Beth Elohim's abandonment of Orthodox Judaism and turn toward the new Reform Movement. Nearly half of Beth Elohim's members withdrew and organized a new Orthodox congregation, Shearith Israel. This congregation followed the Spanish & Portuguese ritual.

By the year 1850 Charleston, like other cities in the United States, began to receive an influx of Orthodox Jews from Germany and Eastern Europe whose everyday language was German or Yiddish. These Ashkenazic Jews were not comfortable in the Sephardic Shearith Israel Congregation and organized "Brith Sholom" Congregation in 1854. Brith Sholom held services in a house on St. Philip Street, near Calhoun Street. They built their synagogue on the same site in 1874. It was designed in brick and wood, forty

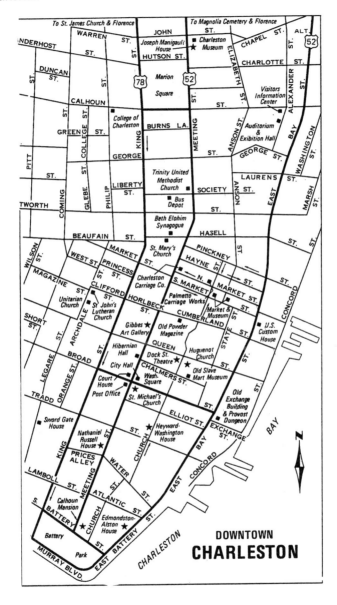

DOWNTOWN
CHARLESTON

feet in front and sixty in depth, two stories high. The architectural style was Tuscan. The galleries rested on fluted iron columns. The Ark, with its ornamented Corinthian pillars, was a gift from Congregation Beth Elohim. The Ten Commandment tablets set above the Ark were presented by the synagogue of Columbia, South Carolina. Brith Sholom was the foremost Orthodox congregation in the South.

In April, 1861 Confederate troops opened fire on Fort Sumter in Charleston Harbor, thereby beginning the War Between the States. The blockade and subsequent siege by Northern troops brought hard times to the Jewish community. Many members left the city during the war years. Nonetheless, the synagogue kept its doors open throughout the four-year long blockade and siege of Charleston. Brith Sholom was the only one of Charleston's three synagogues to function during the War. The members of Brith Sholom furnished a full complement of soldiers for the Confederate Army during the four years of conflict.

During the early 1900s, Jewish immigration to Charleston reached unprecedented levels. It was during this period that tensions and rivalries tended to develop between the more established and those who were recent immigrants. This dissension finally resulted in the founding of a new Orthodox synagogue in Charleston in the spring of 1911 — Beth Israel Congregation. They bought a small building on St. Philip Street but later, in 1947 built an impressive new synagogue on Rutledge Avenue.

In October, 1954, exactly one hundred years after Brith Sholom's founding, Brith Sholom merged with Beth Israel. It was decided to incorporate the imposing interior of Brith Sholom of the century-old St. Philip Street building into the new house of worship.

CAMDEN

BERNARD M. BAURCH HOME
1205 Broad Street

The plaque in front of this Historic Landmark states: On this site stood the birthplace and boyhood home of Bernard M. Baruch (1870-1965), financier, philanthropist, and advisor to presidents. He was instrumental in establishing the Camden Hospital, which opened in 1913, as a tribte to his father, Dr. Simon Baruch, surgeon in the Confederate Army and later a pioneer in medicine in New York.

COLUMBIA

CONGREGATION BETH SHOLOM (Former)
1000 Hampton Street

Originally built in 1907, Congregation Beth Sholom sold its building in 1936 to a black nightclub known as the Big Apple. A dance by this name originated here and soon swept the country, inspiring the song, "The Big Apple," which was recorded by Tommy Dorsey's orchestra. "The Big Apple" became a best-selling hit in September of 1937. The building is still extant, has been restored, and is not presently being used, although the City of Columbia is attempting to find a tenant. The address of the building before it was moved was 1318 Park Street; it is now 1000 Hampton Street and is located in the heart of the city near convention hotels.

COLUMBIA HEBREW BENEVOLENT SOCIETY
Taylor and Green Streets

This society has been in continuous existence since its organization in 1882. It was chartered in 1834. Its charities are administered to the needs of the community without regard to creed or race. Jews first settled in Columbia in 1786 when the city became the state capital. The city's first synagogue was destroyed by fire when General Sherman bombarded Columbia in 1865.

CEMETERY OF THE COLUMBIA HEBREW BENEVOLENT SOCIETY
Corner of Gasden and Richland Streets

In this cemetery, 2½ blocks south on Gasden Street, are buried many distinguished Jewish citizens, including two mayors of Columbia: Mordecai Hendricks DeLeon (1791-1849) and Henry Lyons (1805-1858).

SYNAGOGUES

[Note: All area codes 803]

Aiken   29801   Congregation Adath Jeshurun (R)   *Greenville Street*   649-6301

Anderson   29621   Temple B'nai Israel (C)   *Oakland Avenue* 226-0310

Beaufort   29902   Congregation Beth Israel (C)   *306 East Street*   524-4076

Charleston   29401   Congregation Brith Sholom-Beth Israel (O)   *182 Rutledge Avenue*   577-6599
Synagogue Emanu-El (C)   *5 Windsor Drive*   571-3264
Kahal Kadosh Beth Elohim (R)   *90 Hasell Street*   723-1090

Columbia   29211   Congregation Beth Sholom (C)
5827 North Trenholm Road   782-2500
Tree of Life Congregation (R)   *2701 Heyward Street* 799-2485

Florence   29501   Temple Beth Israel (R)   *316 Park Avenue* 669-9724

Georgetown   29440   Temple Beth Elohim (R)   *Screven Street*   546-7925

Greenville   29602   Beth Israel Synagogue (C)   *425 Summit Drive*   232-9031
Temple of Israel (R)   *115 Buist Avenue*   233-2421

Kingstree   29556   Temple Beth Or (C)   *107 Hirsch Street* 354-6425

Spartanburg   29302   Congregation B'nai Israel (C)
146 Heywood Avenue   582-2001

Sumter   29150   Congregation Sinai (R)   *11 Church Street* 773-2122

THE OLD NEIGHBORHOODS

The following list contains information about synagogues which are no longer functioning as Jewish houses of worship. These addresses are located in the old sections of the city or town. It is advisable to take extra precautions while driving through these neighborhoods.

Aiken   Congregation Adath Jeshurun   *900 Greenville Street, N.W.*

Beaufort   Congregation Beth Israel   *Scott Street Craven Street*

Charleston   Congregation Brith Sholom   *64 St. Philip Street*
Congregation Beth Israel   *182½ Rutledge Street*
Synagogue Emanu-El   *78 Gordon Street*
Hebrew Congregation   *20 Thomas Street*

Columbia   Congregation Beth Sholom   *1318 Park Street 1719 Marion Street*

Dillon   Congregation Ohav Sholom   *10th & Calhoun Streets*

Georgetown   Temple Beth Elohim   *High & Market Streets*

Greenville   Beth Israel Synagogue   *307 Townes Street*

Kingstree   Temple Beth Or   *107 Brockington Street*

Myrtle Beach   Temple Emanu-El   *65th Street, North*

Orangeburg   Temple Sinai   *800 Ellis Avenue, N.E.*

Rock Hill   Temple Beth El   *100 East Main Street*

Spartanburg   Congregation B'nai Israel   *South Dean Street*

TENNESSEE

The first Jewish settlers in Tennessee arrived in the early 1830s and 1840s. They came north from New Orleans and the river towns of Mississippi, south from St. Louis, and west from Cincinnati and Louisville. The earliest Jewish communities were in Memphis, Nashville, and Chattanooga. The first synagogue, Congregation B'nai Israel, was organized in 1853 in Memphis. Nashville's first synagogue, Congregation B'nai Israel, was organized in 1854. In 1862, a second congregation, B'nai Jeshurun, was organized. Both congregations barely survived the Civil War. Nashville's first synagogue was located in a house on Second Avenue, North, just beyond the L&N Railroad station. The congregation followed the Orthodox ritual. In 1868, B'nai Israel and B'nai Jeshurun merged with a third congregation, Kahal Kodesh Ohavai Sholom, and adopted the Reform ritual. This Vine Street Temple, as it was then called, was dedicated by Rabbi Isaac M. Wise in 1875. Also present at the dedication ceremony was Andrew Johnson, War Governor of Tennessee, and later President of the United States.

Chattanooga's Jewish settlement dates from 1858. The Hebrew Benevolent Society, organized in 1866, later became the Mizpah Congregation. Knoxville's Jewish community was organized around 1864 with the creation of the Hebrew Benevolent Society. In 1877, it changed its name to Temple Beth El but did not build its first synagogue until 1914. One of the leaders of Knoxville's Hebrew Benevolent Society was Julius Ochs. He arrived from Germany in 1845. His son, Adolph Ochs, married the daughter of Dr. Isaac Mayer Wise. In 1899, Ochs became the owner and publisher of the New York Times which was suffering financial difficulties.

On November 9, 1862, five months after the Union forces captured Memphis and proclaimed martial law, General Ulysses S. Grant sent orders that, "No Jews are to be permitted to travel on the railroad southward from any point. They may go north and be encouraged in it; but they are such an intolerable nuisance that the Department of Tennessee must be purged of them." These instructions paved the way for Grant's notorious Order No. 11 decreeing the expulsion of all Jews from the military Department of Tennessee, which included northern Mississippi, and all territory in Kentucky and Mississippi west of the Tennessee River. This infamous order of December 17, 1862, expelled all Jews "as a class" from Tennessee within 24 hours! This drastic decree was part of the Union Army's attempt to halt trading with the Confederacy and the resulting widespread profiteering. Several Jewish community leaders met with President Abraham Lincoln, who promptly rescinded Grant's order.

There were early Jewish settlements in Brownsville, Clarksville, Jackson, and Columbia. The Jewish population of Tennessee is approximately 17,000.

BROWNSVILLE

TEMPLE ADAS ISRAEL
Washington Street

Organized in 1868, Temple Adas Israel has been recently declared a National Historic Landmark.

MEMPHIS

CONGREGATION ANSHEI SPHARD
BETH EL EMETH
120 East Yates Road, North

Tennessee's first synagogue, Congregation B'nai Israel, was or-
ganized in 1854. In 1860, a splinter group organized Beth El
Emeth. In 1904, Anshei Sphard was founded by a group of Polish
immigrants. The first synagogue building was located on Market
Street. It was used until 1948 at which point its building at 1188
North Parkway was constructed. Anshei Sphard remained at that
location until 1970. Beth El Emeth's last location was at 3771
Poplar Avenue (from 1958-1969). Anshei Sphard merged with
Beth El Emeth in 1966.

BARON HIRSCH CONGREGATION
1740 Vollentine Avenue

Named for Baron Maurice de Hirsch, the French Jewish indus-
trialist who contributed millions of dollars for the resettlement of
Russian Jews during the pogroms of the 1880s in South America,
the United States, and Canada. The congregation is said to have
the largest Sanctuary of any Orthodox synagogue in the country.
This synagogue is located in the old section of Memphis and is
used primarily for special occasions such as wedding ceremonies.
The congregation's East Side Educational Center is located at 5631
Shady Grove Road.

TEMPLE ISRAEL
1376 East Massey Road

Tennessee's first congregation was organized in 1854 as Congregation B'nai Israel. It originally followed the Orthodox ritual. In 1860, the congregation moved towards Reform. In 1882, a new temple was built on Poplar Street, between 2nd and 3rd Streets. Its next building was located at Poplar and Montgomery Streets and was dedicated in June, 1915. During the years of World War II, some 400 members of the congregation served in the armed forces, fourteen of whom gave their lives. The closing ceremonies of the Poplar/Montgomery Sanctuary were held in September, 1976. The present modern temple is located on East Massey Road. It was designed by the architectural firm of Gassner, Nathan and Partners with architectural art designed by Efrem Weitzman.

NASHVILLE

CONGREGATION OHABAI SHOLOM
5015 Harding Road

Nashville's first congregation, B'nai Israel, was organized as an Orthodox congregatioin in 1854. Ohabai Sholom was created as an offshoot from that pioneer congregation in 1868. It followed the Reform ritual. Its first synagogue, known as the Vine Street Temple, was dedicated in 1875. Rabbi Isaac Mayer Wise and Andrew Johnson, the former President of the United States, officiated at the ceremonies.

The present temple building of Ohabai Sholom was designed by Braverman and Halperin. There is a limestone sculpture on the façade, designed by Raymond Katz representing Truth, Justice, and

The old Vine Street Temple was dedicated in 1875.

Peace. The artist Ben Shahn designed a magnificent mosaic mural for the vestibule in 1959. It is called "The Call of the Shofar."

OAK RIDGE

JEWISH CONGREGATION OF OAK RIDGE
Madison Lane and Michigan Avenue

This congregation was founded in 1943 by Jewish scientists, technicians, and military personnel to this top secret government installation. It was at Oak Ridge where the first atomic power pile was built. In 1959, the government gave up the Oak Ridge plant and the place became the incorporated City of Oak Ridge.

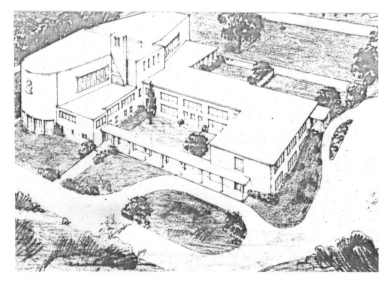

Ohabei Sholom is Nashville's oldest congregation.

SYNAGOGUES

Blountville   37617   Congregation B'nai Sholom (C)
Route 2

Brownsville   38012   Congregation Adas Israel (R)
Washington Street   (901) 772-2407

Chattanooga   37411   Beth Sholom Synagogue (O)
20 Pisgah Avenue   (618) 894-0801
B'nai Zion Synagogue (C)   *114 McBrian Road   894-8900*
Congregation Mizpah (R)   *923 McCarlie Avenue   267-9771*

Jackson   38301   Congregation B'nai Israel (R)   *Campbell &
Grand Streets   (901) 427-6141*

Knoxville   37919   Temple Beth El (R)   *3037 Kingston Pike
(615) 524-3521*
Congregation Heska Amuna (C)   *3811 Kingston Pike
522-0701*

Memphis   38119   Congregation Anshe Sfard Beth El
Emeth (O)
120 East Yates Road, North   (901) 682-1611
Baron Hirsch Synagogue (O)   *400 South Yates Road   683-7485*
Baron Hirsch Synagogue West (O)   *1740 Vollintine Avenue
683-7485*
Congregation Beth Sholom (C)   *482 South Mendelhall Road
683-3591*
Temple Israel (R)   *1376 East Massey Road   761-3130*

Nashville   37205   Congregation Sherith Israel (O)
3600 West End Avenue   (615) 292-6614
The Temple (R)   *5015 Harding Road   352-7620*
West End Synagogue (C)   *3814 West End Avenue   269-4592*

Oak Ridge   37830   Jewish Congregation (C)   *Madison Lane
& Michigan Avenue   (615) 483-3581*

THE OLD NEIGHBORHOODS

The following list contains information about synagogues which are no longer functioning as Jewish houses of worship. These addresses are located in the old sections of the city or town. It is advisable to take extra precautions while driving through these neighborhoods.

Bristol B'nai Sholom Congregation *820 Southside Avenue*

Chattanooga B'nai Zion Synagogue 534 Vine Street
Congregation Mizpah *Walnut Street, between 5th & 6th Streets*
Shaari Zion Congregation *99 Thalley Road*

Jackson Congregation B'nai Israel *College & Hurt Streets*
32 Russell Road
401 West Grand Avenue

Knoxville Temple Beth El *623 West Vine Street*
Congregation Heska Amuna *529 West 5th Street*
Masry Street

Memphis Congregation Anshe Sfard Beth El Emeth
Market Street
165 Poplar Avenue
1188 North Parkway
3771 Poplar Avenue
Baron Hirsch Synagogue *Washington & 4th Streets*
Temple Israel *Montgomery Street*
Congregation B'nai Israel *Poplar Street, between 2nd & 3rd Streets*
Poplar & Montgomery Streets

Nashville Congregation Ohabai Sholom *136 7th Avenue*
Vine Street

Union City Jewish Center *100 South Home Street*

VIRGINIA

One of the earliest known Jews in Virginia was John de Sequerya, a doctor who kept his religion a secret. A *Marrano* (secret Jew) who was born in London, de Sequerya came to Williamsburg in 1745 where he began the practice of medicine. On several occasions he treated George Washington's step-daughter, Patsy Custus. Thomas Jefferson credited Dr. Sequeyra with having introduced the tomato as a vegetable to the Colonies.

Other early Jewish settlers include Isaacs and Cohen, who dealt in slaves, owned Richmond's oldest tavern, *The Bird-in-Hand,* and specialized in land warrants, which had been used by the states to pay their debts to the troops who had served in the Revolution. They commissioned Daniel Boone to locate and explore 10,000 acres in Kentucky. Isaacs noted in Yiddish the transaction with Daniel Boone on the back of the receipts.

During the American Revolution, Simon Nathan, an English Jew who was in business in Jamaica, smuggled war supplies from the West Indies to Virginia by way of neutral ports.

Virginia's first congregation, Kahal Kodesh Beth Shalome, was organized in Richmond on August 24, 1789. It was the sixth oldest congregation in the United States. In 1848, the first synagogue building was constructed. It was located on 11th Street between Clay and Marshall Streets. One of the founders of Beth Shalome, Moses Myers, moved to Norfolk in 1800. He became wealthy as an importer, became the Norfolk Superintendent of the Bank of Richmond, acted as Thomas Jefferson's personal agent, served in the City Council, and served as Collector of the Port of Norfolk from 1827-1831.

Congregation Beth Shalome's services followed the Sephardic Orthodox ritual. Most of its members, in later years however, were

Ashkenazic Jews of German origin. In 1839, Chevra Ahabat Yis-
roel was organized in Richmond as a charitable and social society.
Two years later it became Congregation Beth Ahabah. In 1898,
Beth Shalome merged with Beth Ahabah.

Some of the earliest Jewish congregations in Virginia include:
Norfolk's Ohef Sholom (1848) and Beth El (1850); Alexandria's
Beth El Hebrew Congregation (1859); Danville (1877), Petersburg
(1857), and Lynchburg (1867). The Jewish communities in
Roanoke, Newport News, Portsmouth, Staunton, and Fre-
dericksburg were settled in the 1880s.

Several Jews were among the leading slave auctioneers and
slave-trading firms in the South. During the Civil War over 100
Jews from Richmond alone served in the Confederate forces. Congregation Beth Ahabah's religious school, which was suspended
during the Civil War, was used as a makeshift hospital. Almost
every Jewish house served as a military hospital. Southern anti-Se-
mites blamed Jews for inflation, shortage of goods, and other
economic problems. A Jewish colonel, Adolphus H. Adler, offerred
to meet the editor of the *Richmond Examiner* in a duel because
the editor was printing libelous statements about Jews. The editor
ultimately apologized.

The Jewish population of Virginia is approximately 58,700.

ARLINGTON

ARLINGTON NATIONAL CEMETERY

The two most distinguished Jews buried in Arlington National
Cemetery are Sir Moses J. Ezekiel and Brigadier General Charles
H. Launchheimer.

Moses Jacob Ezekiel (1844-1917) was a Jew of Sephardic descent who was born and spent his childhood in Richmond, Virginia. He fought as a Confederate soldier in 1864, graduated from the Virginia Military Institute in 1866, and studied anatomy at the Medical College of Virginia. He moved to Cincinnati which was heavily settled by German immigrants. Ezekiel's fellow artist and friend, Henry Moslar, an American painter of Jewish descent, urged Ezekiel to study in Europe.

In 1869, he was admitted to the Royal Academy of Art in Berlin. After graduating he moved to Rome, Italy where he designed several sculptural reliefs including *Israel and Adam* and *Eve Finding the Body of Cain*. He received his first major sculptural commission in 1873 for *Religious Liberty*. The majestic sculpture was commissioned by the B'nai B'rith for America's centennial celebration in 1876. It is believed to be the first sculpture made by a Jewish artist for a Jewish organization.

The monument, designed in Europe, was too large to be carried in the hold, was shipped to America on the deck of the steamer. Ezekiel unveiled the monument in Philadelphia's Fairmount Park on Thanksgiving Day of 1876. The *Religious Liberty* monument was moved in 1985 and now stands outside the National Museum of American Jewish History in Philadelphia, adjoining Independence Park.

Among Ezekiel's works are busts of Robert E. Lee, Thomas Jefferson, and Stonewall Jackson. He received honorary titles from William II, Emperor of Germany in 1893 and King Victor Emanuel III of Italy in 1906. In 1912, he designed the *New South*, the Monument of Confederate War Dead in Arlington National Cemetery. In 1917, Sir Moses Jacob Ezekiel died in Italy. His body was interred at the foot of the monument which he designed in Arlington, Virginia.

The other Jewish notable buried in Arlington National Cemetery is Brigadier General H. Launchheimer. He was born in Baltimore in 1859 and graduated from the United States Naval Academy in 1883. He was assigned to the Philippines where he established

Sir Moses Jacob Ezekiel during the Civil War.

The New South monument in Arlington National Cemetery.

the office of assistant adjutant and inspector in the Far East. He was later inspector at Marine Corps headquarters. He died in 1920.

CHARLOTTESVILLE

MONTICELLO

Monticello, the home of Thomas Jefferson, located three miles from Charlottesville, was saved from ruin and restored by Uriah P. Levy. Uriah and his beautiful wife, Virginia, of Kingston, Jamaica, lived in the stately Monticello, which he purchased in 1836 for $2,700. Here his marriage took place, and his mother Rachel is buried.

Uriah Phillips Levy entered the United States Navy as a sailing master during the War of 1812 and served on the USS *Argus*, which spread terror among British ships in European waters. At one point Levy was captured and spent sixteen months in England's Dartmoor Prison. His career was marked by six court-martials, mostly for violating regulations. Nevertheless, Levy climbed from the rank of lieutenant in 1817 to the rank of commodore in 1859.

Levy spent most of his shore leave restoring the vandalized architectural masterpiece, Monticello, to its original splendor. In 1923 the home was acquired by the Thomas Jefferson Memorial Foundation as a national shrine. Levy fathered the law for the abolition of corporal punishment in the U.S. Navy, the first Navy in the world to do so, and for which the Commodore Levy Chapel at the Norfolk Naval Base was named. The chapel incidentally has also the unique distinction of being the first permanent Jewish chapel ever built by the U.S. armed forces.

Commodore Uriah P. Levy.

NEWPORT NEWS

ADATH JESHURUN SYNAGOGUE
12646 Nettles Drive

Organized in 1893, Adath Jeshurun built its first synagogue on
Huntington Avenue, near 23rd Street. The first frame structure
was replaced in 1900 by a brick three story building. The next
move, to Madison Avenue and 28th Street, was in 1927. The
adjoining Graff Memorial Building served as the home for the
Hebrew school, Sunday school, meeting rooms, and during the
Second World War it was used as the USO, where many military
men came for a bit of Jewish hospitality.

In 1959, plans were again formulated for a fourth home. The
Stuart Gardens Corporation donated the land at 1815 Chestnut
Avenue. The present home of the congregation, on Nettles Drive,
was completed in September, 1982. The congregation follows the
Orthodox ritual.

Adath Jeshurun Synagogue in Newport News, Virginia.

NORFOLK

COMMODORE LEVY CHAPEL
United States Naval Base

The Levy Chapel is named for the Jewish naval officer, Commodore Uriah Phillips Levy who entered the U.S. navy as a sailing master during the War of 1812 and climbed to the rank of commodore in 1859. It dates from 1943 when it was the first permanent Jewish chapel established on a U.S. military installation. Chaplain Jonathan Panitz leads services for active duty Jewish personnel in the Commodore Levy Chapel. Call 444-7361 for information on visiting.

MOSES MYERS HOUSE
Freemason and Banks Streets

Moses Myers was among other things a ship owner, Collector of the Port of Norfolk, Presidnet of the Common Council, prize master on behalf of the American Navy, and agent of the French Republic.

One of the most elegant early American town houses in existence is the late 18th Century type Georgian home which Moses Myers and his Canadian bride Elizah built in 1791 on Freemason and Banks Streets. The house was owned by the Myers family until 1929 when it was conveyed to the City of Norfolk as part of the Chrysler Museum.

As a Jewish home the Moses Myers House still proudly displays a *mezuzah* on its doorpost. During the holiday of Chanukah the *menorah* is lit in the window as a public testimony of the world's first struggle for religious liberty. The Moses Myers House has been declared an official Historic Landmark.

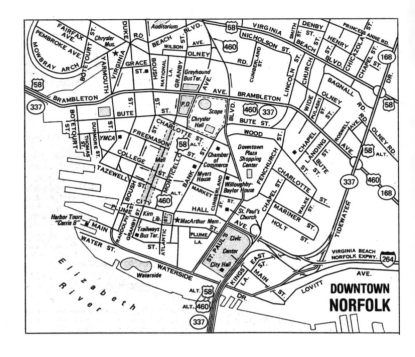

TEMPLE OHEF SHOLOM
530 Raleigh Avenue

The oldest congregation in Norfolk, Ohef Sholom, was founded
in 1848. The first synagogue in the city was built in 1859 on
Cumberland Street. By 1900, three synagogues had been established in the Norfolk/Berkley area and its congregations delineated:
a Reform synagogue, Ohef Sholom, composed of German-born
Jews and their descendents; a Conservative synagogue, Beth El,
composed mainly of German-born Jews and their descendents who
conserved the more Orthodox ritual of German Jewry; and an
Orthodox synagogue, B'nai Israel, composed of recently arrived

Orthodox Jewish immigrants from Russia, especially Lithuania.

By 1900, Ohef Sholom had for over two decades been located at the former building of the Methodist Protestant Church, situated on 323-25 Church Street. Beth El's house of worship had been in use since 1880. Originally built in 1860 for the Ohef Sholom Congregation and used by them in the 1860s and 1870s, it was located at 157-63 Cumberland Street just opposite the Norfolk Academy.

The recently arrived East European "Russian" Jewish immigrants generally belonged to the Orthodox synagogue, B'nai Israel. Established around 1897, it acquired a building at 194 Cumberland Street in 1898, but by 1901 it would purchase a more permanent location further below on the same street (13-21 Cumberland Street).

On May 23, 1902, Temple Ohef Sholom dedicated its new building at Freemason and Tripoli (today Monticello) Streets. It was designed by the architectural firm of Peebles & Associates. The edifice measured about 80 feet square, and in architectural design was of the Italian Renaissance type. The structure was two

Ohef Sholom's first building was located at 157 Cumberland Street.

stories in height and was constructed of light pressed brick, with
terra cotta and limestone trimming. The building was surmounted
with five copper-covered domes — one main and four subordinate.
The main dome was 40 feet in diameter. The site and synagogue.
with furnishings complete, cost between $65,000 and $70,000.

The present location of these three congregations are: Ohef
Sholom Temple — 530 Raleigh Avenue; Congregation Beth El —
422 Shirley Avenue; and B'nai Israel Congregation — 420
Spotswood Avenue.

Temple Ohef Sholom is Norfolk's oldest congregation.

OLDEST JEWISH CEMETERY
Princess Anne Road and Tidewater Drive

In 1817, the death of a Jewish resident prompted the establishment
of Norfolk's Jews' Cemetery in Washington Point (later known
as Berkley). The early 1840s brought the great wave of German
Jews into the country. The first congregation, Chevra B'nai Jacob,
was organized in 1848. It later became the Ohef Sholom Temple.
In 1850, another Jewish cemetery was established, on Princess
Anne Road; known as the Hebrew Cemetery, it is still in use today.

Cantor Iser Learman of Norfolk and his family, ca. 1914.

RICHMOND

SITE OF JUDAH P. BENJAMIN RESIDENCE
9 West Main Street

A stone marker in the sidewalk marks the site of the residence of Judah P. Benjamin during the Civil War, when he served as Secretary of War and Secretary of State of the Confederacy.

CONGREGATION BETH AHABAH
1117 West Franklin Street

Virginia's oldest congregation, Kahal Kodesh Beth Shalome, was organized in 1789. It was the sixth oldest congregation in the United States. The congregation, at its start, was Orthodox and followed the Sephardic ritual. In 1841, an Ashkenazic congregation, Beth Ahabah, was organized by German Jews. In 1898, these two congregations merged and kept the name Beth Ahabah. The congregation now follows the Reform ritual.

FIRST JEWISH CEMETERY IN VIRGINIA
Franklin Street, West of 21st Street

Above the gate surrounding the Franklin Street Burying Ground is a sign, "The First Jewish Cemetery in Virginia." The cemetery was established by Congregation Beth Shalome, Virginia's oldest synagogue, in 1791. In 1817, the Hebrew Cemetery, located at 5th and Hospital Streets, replaced the old Franklin Street Burying

Grounds. The Hebrew Cemetery contains the remains of a number of Confederate soldiers.

Beth Ahabah is Virginia's oldest congregation.

STAUNTON

TEMPLE HOUSE OF ISRAEL
19 North Market Street

Temple House of Israel was organized in 1876 under the leadership of Alexander Hart, a former major in the Confederate Army. Major Hart became the first President of the congregation.

The first permanent house of worship was purchased in 1885. The building, located at 200 Kalorama Street, known then as the Hoover School, still stands and today houses an upholstery shop. The congregation puchased a lot on North Market Street from Mary Baldwin College. S.J. Collins, a local architect, was engaged to design the new building which they first occupied in 1925. The building has been in continuous use since then. The congregation follows the Reform ritual.

SYNAGOGUES

Alexandria   22302   Agudas Achim Congregation (C)
2908 Valley Drive   *(703) 548-4122*
Beth El Hebrew Congregation (R)   *3830 Seminary Road*
370-9400

Arlington   22204   Arlington-Fairfax Jewish Congregation (C)
2920 Arlington Boulevard   *(703) 979-4466*

Charlottesville   22902   Temple Beth Israel (R)   *301 East
Jefferson Street*   *(804) 295-6382*

Fairfax   22031   Congregation Olam Tikvah (C)
3800 Glenbrook Road   *(703) 425-1880*

Falls Church   22043   Temple Rodef Sholom (R)
2100 Westmorland Street   *(703) 532-2217*

Fredericksburg   Beth Sholom Temple (R)   *515 Charlotte
Street*   *(703) 373-4834*

Hampton   23661   B'nai Israel Synagogue (T)
3116 Kecoughtan Road   *(804) 722-0100*
Temple Rodef Sholom (C)   *318 Whealton Road*   *826-5894*

Harrisonburg   22801   Temple Beth El (R)   *Old Furnace
Road*   *(703) 434-2744*

Lynchburg   24501   Agudath Sholom Congregation (R)
2055 Langhorne Road   *(804) 846-0739*

Martinsville   24112   Congregation Ohev Zion (R)
801 Parkview Avenue   *(703) 632-2828*

Newport News   23607   Congregation Adath Jeshurun (O)
12646 Nettles Drive   *(804) 599-0820*
Temple Sinai (R)   *11620 Warwick Boulevard*   *596-8352*

Norfolk   23517   Congregation Beth El (C)   *422 Shirley
Avenue*   *(804) 625-7821*
Congregation B'nai Israel (O)   *420 Spotswood Avenue*
627-7358

Temple Israel (C)   *7255 Granby Street*   *489-4550*
Temple Ohef Sholom (R)   *530 Raleigh Avenue*   *625-4295*

Petersburg   23803   Congregation Brith Achim (C)
314 South Boulevard   *(804) 732-3968*

Portsmouth   23703   Congregation Chevre Tehillim (O)
Effingham & High Streets   *(804) 399-3963*
Congregation Gomley Chesed (C)   *3110 Sterling Point Drive*
(804) 484-1019
Temple Sinai (R)   *4401 Hatton Point Drive*   *484-1730*

Reston   22090   Congregation Beth Emeth (C)   *1441 Wiehler Drive*   *(703) 860-4515*

Richmond   23220   Congregation Beth Ahaba (R)
1117 West Franklin Street   *(804) 358-6757*
Temple Beth El (C)   *3330 Grove Avenue*   *355-3564*
Temple Rodef Sholom   *318 Wheaton Road*   *826-5894*
Congregation B'nai Sholom (C)   *9500 Three Chopt Road*   *270-7011*
Knesseth Beth Israel Congregation (O)   *6300 Patterson Avenue*   *288-7953*
Congregation Kol Emes (O)   *4811 Patterson Avenue*   *353-5831*
Congregation Or Ami (R)   *3406 Huguenot Road*   *272-0017*

Roanoke   24016   Congregation Beth Israel (C)
920 Franklin Road, S.W.   *(703) 343-0289*
Temple Emanu-El (R)   *1163 Persinger Road, S.W.*   *342-3378*

Staunton   24401   Temple House of Israel (R)   *19 North Market Street*   *(703) 886-4091*

Suffolk   Agudath Achim Congregation   *132 Bank Street*   *539-5342*

Virginia Beach   23458   Beth Chaverim Congregation (R)
4853 Princess Anne Road   *(804) 495-6130*
Temple Emanu-El (C)   *25th Street & Baltic Avenue*   *428-2591*
Congregation Kehilat Bet Hamedrash (C)   *4937 Providence Road*   *495-8510*
Lubavitch Center (O)   *372 South Independence Boulevard*   *490-9699*

Williamsburg Temple Beth El *600 Jamestown Road*
220-1205
Woodbridge 22194 Congregation Ner Tamid (R)
2481 Longview Drive (703) 494-3251

THE OLD NEIGHBORHOODS

The following list contains information about synagogues which are no longer functioning as Jewish houses of worship. These addresses are located in the old sections of the city or town. It is advisable to take extra precautions while driving through these neighborhoods.

Alexandria Agudas Achim Congregation *1400 Russel Road*
Beth El Hebrew Congregation *206 North Washington Street*
Arlington Jewish Congregation *Lee Boulevard*
Berkeley Congregation Mikdash Kodesh *Market & 11th Street*
Rockingham & Liberty Streets
Bristol Temple B'nai Sholom *King & 2nd Streets*
Bluefield Congregation Ahavath Sholom *Albermarle Street*
Charlottesville Temple Beth Israel *Market Street*
Chesapeake Congregation Gomley Chesed *220 Sterling Point Drive*
Danville Congregation Aetz Chayim *728 Wilson Street*
168 Stratford Place
Beth Sholom Temple *127 Sutherland Avenue*
Fairfax Magen David Congregation *9112 Bowler Drive*
Falls Church Temple Rodef Sholom *515 Charlotte Street*

Hampton   B'nai Israel Congregation   *18 Locust Avenue*
Harrisonburg   Temple Beth El   *234 North Main Street*
Lynchburg   Agudath Sholom Congregation   *513 Church Street*
15 Riverview Place
Martinsville   Congregation Ohev Zion   *Moss Street*
Newport News   Congregation Adath Jeshurun   *28th & Madison Streets*
1815 Chestnut Avenue
Huntington Avenue, near 23rd Street
Norfolk   Congregation Beth El   *422 West 15th Street*
157 Cumberland Street
Congregation B'nai Israel   *194 Cumberland Street*
Temple Ohef Sholom   *323 Church Street*
Freemason & Tripoli Streets
157 Cumberland Street
Petersburg   Congregation Brith Achim   *Market Street*
Temple Rodef Sholom   *South Sycamore Street*
Portsmouth   Congregation Gomley Chesed   *County Street*
Richmond   Congregation B'nai Sholom   *6007 West Club Lane*
6209 Patterson Avenue
Knesseth Beth Israel Congregation   *Mayo Street, between Broad & Ross Street*
Beth Shalome   *11th Street, between Clay & Marshall Streets*
Congregation Or Ami   *5400 Monument Avenue*
Beth Israel Congregation   *Grove Avenue & North Boulevard*
Congregation Etz Chaim   *4501 Patterson Avenue*
Beth Torah Congregation   *Floyd Avenue*
Staunton   Temple House of Israel   *315 North New Street*
303 Alpine Road
Market & Kalorama Streets
Suffolk   Congregation Agudath Achim   *132 Bank Street*
Winchester   Beth El Congregation   *528 Fairmont Avenue*

WEST VIRGINIA

All of what is now West Virgina, was part of Virginia until 1863. Only after Wheeling and Charleston became important trading towns in the 1830s and 1840s, did Jews begin settling there, coming as pack paddlers from Baltimore and Pittsburgh.

The oldest Jewish community of West Virginia is in Wheeling, where the first Jewish organization in the state, a Chevre Kadischa or cemetery association, was organized in 1849 and a burial ground was acquired in Mt. Wood Cemetery. The first to be laid to rest in the cemetery was Rabbi Meyer Mannheim, the rabbi of the Jewish community. Congregation Leshem Shomayim was organized as an Orthodox congregation. It became a charter member of the Union of American Hebrew Congregations and adopted the Reform ritual. The first synagogue, known as the Eoff Street Temple, was completed in 1891. This temple was later demolished and replaced by the Woodsdale Temple, which was dedicated on April 18, 1958.

In 1926, a Conservative congregation, Synagogue of Israel, was organized. In 1974, Synagogue of Israel and the Eoff Street Temple merged and changed the name of the congregation to Temple Shalom. Today, Temple Shalom is a Reform congregation with traditional leaning. The original building of Synagogue of Israel, located at 115½ Edginton Lane, is now used for offices of Gompers and Company, Certified Public Accountants.

There were less than 500 Jews in West Virginia after the Civil War. There was an attempt to locate the Union of American Hebrew Congregations in Charleston, West Virginia as well as the Hebrew Union College. The City of Cincinnati, Ohio was selected ultimately as the home of both the Hebrew Union College and the Union of American Hebrew Congregations in 1873.

There were additional Jewish settlements in Bluefield (1880), Mount Hope (1895), Fairmont (1899), and Clarksburg (1903). Because so much of West Virginia's economy was based on coal, some of the towns and cities lost population, including Jews, when oil gradually replaced coal as the country's major fuel.

The Jewish population of West Virginia is approximately 3,800.

CHARLESTON

CONGREGATION B'NAI ISRAEL
2312 Kanawha Boulevard East

The first Jewish congregation in Charleston was founded in 1873 under the name of the Hebrew Educational Society. The first services were held in rooms over a store on Capitol Street. The Union of American Hebrew Congregations was organized that same year in Cincinnati and the congregation was one of the original 34 members. In 1875, the congregation moved to a small temple on State Street, now Lee Street.

The Virginia Street Temple was erected and dedicated in 1894. Dr. Isaac Mayer Wise delivered the dedicatory sermon. This building served the congregation for 66 years. The present edifice, located on Kanawha Boulevard at Chesapeake Avenue, was completed in 1960.

Isaac Ochs of Wheeling, West Virginia, was an officer in the Union Army.

The Eoff Street Temple was built in 1891.

WHEELING

TEMPLE SHALOM
23 Bethany Pike

The oldest synagogue in West Virginia was organized in 1849 as Congregation Leshem Shomayim. The former Eoff Street Temple, built in 1891, was demolished and replaced by the Woodsdale Temple. In 1974, the Conservative Synagogue of Israel merged with the Reform Woodsdale Temple and changed its name to Temple Shalom. The congregation now follows the Reform ritual with traditional leaning.

SYNAGOGUES

[Note: All area codes 304]

Beckley   25801   Temple Beth El (R)   107 *Queen Street*
253-9421

Bluefield   24701   Congregation Ahavath Sholom (R)
632 Albermarle Street   *325-9372*

Charleston   25311   Congregation B'nai Jacob (T)
1599 Virginia Street   *344-4167*
Temple Israel (R)   *2312 Kanawha Boulevard*   *342-5852*

Clarksburg   26301   Tree of Life Synagogue (C)   *425 West*
Pike Street

Huntington   25720   B'nai Sholom Congregation (C)
949 10th Avenue   *522-2980*
Ohev Sholom Congregation (R)   *900 9th Street*

Logan   25601   Congregation B'nai El (R)   *651 Stratton Street*

Martinsburg   25401   Congregation Beth Jacob (R)
126 West Martin Street   *267-6824*

Morgantown   26505   Tree of Life Congregation (R)
242 South High Street   *292-7029*

Welch   24801   Congregation Emanu-El (R)   *Riverside Drive*
436-4768

Wheeling   26003   Temple Sholom (R)   *23 Bethany Pike*
233-4870

Williamson   25661   Temple B'nai Israel (R)   *College Hill*
235-2947

THE OLD NEIGHBORHOODS

The following list contains information about synagogues which are no longer functioning as Jewish houses of worship. These addresses are located in the old sections of the city or town. It is advisable to take extra precautions while driving through these neighborhoods.

Charleston   Bene Jeshurun Congregation   *State Street*
Virginia Street
Fairmont   Temple Beth El   *405 4th Street*
Huntington   B'nai Sholom Congregation   *1203 10th Avenue*
Ohev Sholom Synagogue   *949 10th Avenue*
Parkersburg   B'nai Israel Temple   *1703 20th Street*
646 7th Street
Weirton   Congregation Beth Israel   *500 Brookline Drive*
Wheeling   Temple Sholom   *12th & Eoff Streets*
Synagogue of Israel   *115½ Edginton Lane*

KOSHER RESTAURANTS & EATERIES

ALABAMA

Birmingham Browdy's 2807 Cahaba Road
(205) 879-8585
Pizizt Bake Shop 600 Brookwood Village (205) 322-9602
Mobile Schwartz's Deli 53 South Georgia Avenue
(205) 432-0891

ARKANSAS

Little Rock Andre's 11121 Rodney Parham Road
(501) 224-7880

FLORIDA

Deerfield Beach Star of David Supermarket
1806 West Hillsboro Boulevard (305) 427-6400
Sara's 1898 West Hillsboro Boulevard 427-2272
Delray Beach Fiddler's 14802 Military Trail
(305) 498-0090
Fort Lauderdale Harrison's Kosher Meat Market
8330 West Oakland Park Boulevard (305) 741-0855
Tom-Tov Kosher Butcher & Appetizer 2610 West
Atlantic Avenue (305) 741-1995
Hallandale Embassy Kosher Steak House
1025 East Hallandale Beach Boulevard
(305) 456-7550

Lauderhill   Kosher Treats   *5524 West Oakland Park Boulevard*   *(305) 731-6200*

Margate   East Side Deli   *6846 West Atlantic Boulevard*   *(305) 971-8340*

Miami Beach

Dairy Delights   *3925 Collins Avenue*   *531-8383* *(Cadillac Hotel)*

Dine or Nosh   *420 41st Street*   *538-9104*

Embassy 41 Deli   *534 41st Street*   *534-7550*

Kosher Corner   *2701 Collins Avenue*   *674-9222*

Peking Embassy   *1417 Washington Avenue*   *538-7550*

Royal Hungarian   *3925 Collins Avenue*   *532-8566* *(Cadillac Hotel)*

Shloime's Pizza   *753 41st Street*   *538-7333*

Tottie's   *6345 Collins Avenue*   *866-8851* *(Casablanca Hotel)*

Tower 41   *4101 Pinetree Drive*   *673-8308*

North Miami Beach

Jerusalem Pizza   *761 N.E. 167th Street*   *653-6662*

Sara's   *2214 N.E. 123rd Street*   *891-3312*

Golan's   *175 Sunny Isles Boulevard*   *947-4781*

Pastry Lane   *1688 N.E. 164th Street*

Orlando   Palm Terrace   *Hyatt Orlando*
   (305) 396-1234

   Mickey Shalom/Holiday Inn Altamonte Springs
      230 W. Highway 436 (1-4 and State Road 436)
      Altamonte Springs, Florida 32701 800-6-Fla-SUN
      or 305-862-4455

Tampa   Tampa Kosher Meat   *2305 Morrison Avenue*
   (813) 253-5993

GEORGIA

Atlanta   Quality Kosher Meat Market   *2161 Briarcliff Road, N.E.   (404) 636-1114*
Arthur's Kosher Meat Market   *2166 Briarcliff Road (404) 634-6881*
Savannah   Gottlieb's Bakery   *1601 Bull Street (912) 236-4261*

LOUISIANA

Metairie   Lakeshore Hebrew Day School (Food Coop)   *5210 West Esplanade Avenue   (504) 885-4532*
New Orleans   Ralph's Kosher Deli   *4518 Freret Street (504) 891-8476*

NORTH CAROLINA

Charlotte   Phil's Deli   *198 South Sharon Amity Road (704) 366-5405*
Raleigh   Congregation Shaarei Israel (grocery)   *7400 Falls of the Neuse Road   (919) 847-8986*

SOUTH CAROLINA

CHARLESTON   Lash Meat Market   *1107 King Street (803) 577-6501*

TENNESSEE

Memphis   Kipper's Kosher Food   *4965 Summer Avenue*
(901) 682-3801
Samovar Bakery   *5068 Park Avenue*   761-2898
Posh Nosh   *6560 Poplar Avenue*   761-0810
Herby's Bake Shop   *258 Bethel Road*   525-1710

VIRGINIA

Fairfax   Knish-Knosh   *9432 Main Street*   (703) 978-3300
Newport News   Warwick Bakery   *240 31st Street*
(804) 244-1362
Norfolk   Sabra Deli   *7862 Tide Water Drive*   (804) 480-1300
Richmond   Siegel's   *1911 West Main Street*
(804) 233-9627

WEST VIRGINIA

Huntington   Victor's Deli   *625 8th Street*   (304) 522-4123

Chabad Houses

ALABAMA

Birmingham 35223 Rabbi Y.M. Lipszyc *3340 Overton Road* *(205) 328-6724* *(205) 967-4597*

FLORIDA

Clearwater 33515 Rabbi S. Sawilowsky *1995 Byram Drive* *(813) 442-6587*

Coral Springs 33065 Rabbi Y. Denburg *9791 Sample Road* *(305) 344-4855* *(305) 755-9153*

Hallandale 33009 Rabbi R. Tenenhaus *1295 East Hallandale Beach Road* *(305) 458-1877* *(305) 456-7079*

Kissimee 32741 Rabbi Z. Berkowitz *4311 West Vine Street* *(305) 396-4213*

Lauderhill 33321 *4561 North University Drive* *(305) 742-4224*

Maitland 32751 Rabbi S. Dubow (Chabad of Orlando) *2021 Mohawk Terrace* *(305) 740-8770*

Miami Beach 33139 Rabbi A. Korf *1140 Alton Road* *(305) 673-5983*

North Miami Beach 33180 Rabbi K. Brusowankin *2590 N.E. 202nd Street* *(305) 932-7770*

Sarasota   33580   Rabbi A. Bukiet   *230 North Briggs Avenue*
(305) 955-1447
Tampa   33624   Rabbi Y. Dubrowski   *4703 Foxshire Circle*
(813) 963-2317   (813) 962-2375

GEORGIA

Atlanta   30342   Rabbi Y. New   *5065 High Point Road*
(404) 843-2464   (404) 255-7155

LOUISIANA

New Orleans   70118   Rabbi Z. Rivkin   *7073 Freret Street*
(504) 866-5164   (504) 866-5342

NORTH CAROLINA

CHARLOTTE   28226   Rabbi Y. Groner
6500 Newhall Road   (704) 366-3984

SOUTH CAROLINA

Myrtle Beach   29755   Rabbi D. Aizenman
6310 Hawthorne Lane   (803) 449-4832   (803) 449-3956

TENNESSEE

Nashville   37205   Rabbi Z. Posner   *3730 Whitland
Avenue*   (615) 292-6614   (615) 385-3730

VIRGINIA

Fairfax 22031   Rabbi Y. Bula   *3924 Persimmon Drive*
(703) 323-0233
Newport News 23606   Rabbi M. Gurkov   *12646 Nettles Drive   (804) 599-0820   (804) 596-6174*
Richmond 23233   Rabbi Y. Kranz   *212 Gaskins Road*
(804) 740-2000   (804) 741-1000

MIKVEHS

ALABAMA

Birmingham   Knesseth Israel Congregation
3225 Montevallo Road   (205) 879-1664
Montgomery   Congregation Agudath Israel   *3525 Cloverdale
Road   (205) 281-7394*

ARKANSAS

Little Rock   Congregation Agudath Achim   *7901 West 5th
Street   (501) 225-1683 or 225-1667*

FLORIDA

Hollywood   Young Israel   *3291 Stirling Road
(305) 983-5568*
Jacksonville   Eitz Chaim Synagogue
5864 University Boulevard West   (904) 733-0720
Miami   Miami Mikveh   *16260 S.W. 288th Street
(305) 264-6488 or 245-8594*
Miami Beach   Daughters of Israel   *151 Michigan Avenue
(305) 672-3500*

Mikveh Blima of North Dade   *1054 Miami Gardens Drive*
(305) 949-9650

Tampa   Chabad Lubavitch   *3620 Fletcher Avenue*
(813) 971-6768

GEORGIA

Atlanta   Congregation Beth Jacob   *1855 La Vista Road*
(404) 633-0551 *or* 325-3595

Augusta   Congregation Adas Yeshurun   *935 Johns Road*
(404) 733-9491

Savannah   Congregation B'nai B'rith Jacob   *108 Atlas Street*
(404) 355-3406

LOUISIANA

New Orleans   Congregation Beth Israel   *7000 Canal Street*
(504) 866-3716 *or* 288-8943

NORTH CAROLINA

Charlotte   Lubavitch of North Carolina   *6500 Newhall
Road*   (704) 366-3984

Durham   Beth El Congregation   *1004 Watt Street*
(919) 682-1238

Raleigh   Shaarei Israel Congregation   *7400 Falls of the Neuse
Road*   (919) 848-9102

SOUTH CAROLINA

Charleston   Congregation Brith Sholom—Beth Israel
182 Rutledge Avenue   (803) 577-6599

TENNESSEE

Chattanooga   Beth Sholom Congregation   *20 Pisgah
Avenue*   (618) 894-8870
Memphis   Congregation Anshe Sphard   *120 East Yates
Road N.*   (901) 682-1611
Baron Hirsch Mikveh   *1740 Vollintine Avenue*
(901) 683-7485
Nashville   Congregation Sherith Israel   *3600 West end
Avenue*   (615) 385-3730

VIRGINIA

Newport News   Congregation B'nai Israel   *420 Spotswood
Avenue*   (804) 625-4409
Richmond   Congregation Kol Emes   *4811 Patterson Avenue*
(804) 358-3715 *or* 288-4381

WEST VIRGINIA

Charleston   Congregation B'nai Jacob   *1599 Virginia Street*
(304) 344-4167

Israeli Folk Dancing

FLORIDA

Miami   South Dade JCC   *1242 S.W. 102nd Street*
Monday 7:30-9:00 p.m.   *Yossi Yanich*   *(305) 685-1783*
North Miami Beach   McDonald Center   *17051 N.E. 19th Avenue*
Wednesday 8:00-10:30 p.m.   *Miriam Weiner*   *(305) 652-9738*
Congregation Beth Torah   *1051 North Miami Beach Boulevard*
Thursday 7:30-9:00 p.m.   *Yossi Yanich*   *(305) 685-1783*
JCC of North Miami Beach   *19000 25th Avenue*
Sunday 8:00-10:30 p.m.   *Ya'acov Sassi*   *(305) 652-9738*
Gainesville   Dora Freedman   *(904) 377-4745*
Jacksonville   Joan Levin   *(904) 733-1407*   *(904) 241-0501*

GEORGIA

Atlanta   Atlanta JCC   *1745 Peachtree Street*
Wednesday 7:30-10:30 p.m.   *Ken Avner*   *(404) 875-7881*
Emory University (Alumni Memorial Center)
Sunday 7:30-10:00 p.m.   *Jeff Hirschorn*   *(404) 872-9010*

NORTH CAROLINA

Hendersonville   Camp Blue Star   Mid-June   contact:
  Blue Star Folk Dance Workshop
  3595 Sheridan Street   Suite 107
  Hollywood, Florida 33021
  (305) 624-2267

VIRGINIA

Virginia   North Virginia JCC   *Little River Pike*
Thursday 8:00-10:00 p.m.   *Joy Newman*
Reston   North Virginia Hebrew Cong.   *1441 Wiehle Avenue*
  Monday 8:30-10:00 p.m.   *Sandy Weiss Sacks*   *(703) 437-7733*

Bibliography

Blake, P. *An American Synagogue for Today and Tomorrow*, New York: Union of American Hebrew Congregations, 1954

Berent, I.M. *History of Tidewater Jewry*, Renewal Magazine, Vol. 3 No. 1 Sept. 4, 1986 United Jewish Federation of Tidewater

de Breffney, R.G. *The Synagogue*, New York: Sheba Publishing, 1978

Glickenstein, N.H. *That Ye May Remember — Congregation Ahavath Chesed 1882-1982*, St. Petersburg: Byron Kennedy & Co. Publishers, 1982

Levy, A.B. *A Short History of Congregation Mickve Israel of Savannah*

Kaplan, J. *A Hundred and Thirty Years of Orthodox Judaism in the Deep South — A Short History of Brith Sholom Beth Israel Congregation* Charleston, South Carolina

Meltzer, M. *The Jews in America — A Picture Album*, Philadelphia: Jewish Publication Society, 1985

Postal, B. & Koppman, L. *American Jewish Landmarks, Vol. II*, New York: Fleet Press, 1977

Wischnitzer, R. *Synagogue Architecture in the United States, History and Interpretation*, Philadelphia: Jewish Publicationi Society, 1955

Encyclopedia Judaica, Jerusalem: Keter Publishing House, 1972

The Universal Jewish Encyclopedia, 1948

Two Hundred Years of American Synagogue Architecture — Catalogue Waltham, Mass.: American Jewish Historical Society, 1976

Tebeau, C.W. *Synagogue in the Central City — Temple Israel of Greater Miami 1922-1972*, Coral Gables: University of Miami Press, 1972

Kerman, Rabbi J. *The Story of Temple B'nai Israel — Natchez, Miss. Ezekiel's Vision: Moses Jacob Ezekiel and the Classical Tradition* — Catalogue Philadelphia: National Museum of American Jewish History, 1985

Historic Brochures & Anniversary Journals:

Temple House of Israel   Staunton, Virginia

Congregation Beth Ahabah   Richmond, Virginia

Adath Jeshurun Synagogue 1893-1983   Newport News, Virginia

Anshei Sphard — Beth El Emeth Congregation   Memphis, Tennessee
United States Dept. of the Interior   Washington, D.C.
State of North Carolina Dept. of Cultural Resources   Raleigh, N.C.
South Carolina Dept. of Archives & History   Columbia, S.C.
The First 100 Years of Kahl Montgomery 1852-1852
Temple Beth Or   Montgomery, Alabama
Congregation B'nai Israel   Little Rock, Arkansas
Spring Hill Avenue Temple   Mobile, Alabama
*A Century of Reverence 1882-1982   Temple Emanu-El
Birmingham, Alabama*
History of Temple Israel   Columbus, Georgia
Centennial of Congregation Children of Israel 1873-1973   Athens, Georgia
Temple Israel   Memphis, Tennessee
Touro Synagogue   New Orleans, Louisiana
Temple Sinai   New Orleans, Louisiana
Beth Israel Congregation   Jackson, Miss.
The Temple — Congregation Ohabai Sholom   Nashville, Tennessee
The Story of Kahal Kodesh Beth Elohim of Charleston, South Carolina
Temple Shalom   Wheeling, West Virginia
Cuban Hebrew Congregation   Miami Beach, Florida

BOAT TOUR
of
JEWISH NEW YORK

Join Oscar Israelowitz, author of "Guide to Jewish N.Y.C.,"
on a fun-filled 3-hour boat tour around Jewish New York. See
such thrilling sites as the Statue of Liberty, Ellis Island, First
Jewish Settlement in New Amsterdam (1654), Castle Garden,
Holocaust Memorial Museum, Lower East Side, Williamsburg,
Jewish Harlem, Yeshiva University, Jewish Theological Semi-
nary, and much more.

For tickets, reservations, and further information
about this special boat tour and walking tours of the
Lower East Side, please call or write to:

Mr. Oscar Israelowitz
P.O. Box 228
Brooklyn, New York 11229

(718) 951 - 7072

Guide to Jewish Europe

Western Europe Edition

This guide is a "must" for the Jewish traveler to Europe with do-it-yourself tours of London, Venice, Paris, Rome, and Amsterdam. There is information on kosher restaurants and hotels, synagogues and mikvehs, Jewish landmarks and museums, youth hostels, and railroad and Sabbath candlelighting timetables.

Paperback 232 pages $11.50

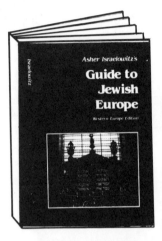

Guide to Jewish U.S.A.

Volume I - The Northeast

The most comprehensive historic and travel guide on Jewish travel in the United States contains information on Jewish historic landmarks, Jewish museums, kosher restaurants, synagogues, mikvehs, and over 100 illustrations.

Paperback 320 pages $11.50

Synagogues of New York City

This pictorial survey of the great synagogues in all five boroughs of New York City contains 123 black and white and color photographs. These photographs outline the history of the Jewish presence in New York City and the role synagogues played in sustaining it. The high quality book makes a fine gift for the Judaica collector.

Paperback 86 pages $7.50

The Lower East Side Guide

This unique guide is designed for the tourist and contains a complete-do-it-yourself walking tour of this historic Jewish neighborhood. It is also designed for the shopper and contains a shopping directory with information on where to find the bargains!

Paperback 124 pages $6.00

Guide to Jewish New York City
1983 Edition

The original 1983 edition contains 10 complete do-it-yourself tours of the largest Jewish city in the world. There are Jewish historic landmarks, Jewish museums, synagogues, kosher restaurants, Israeli folk dancing, and Yiddish theatres.

Paperback 152 pages $3.50

Oscar Israelowitz's
Guide to Jewish New York City

Guide to Jewish New York City
Revised Edition

The expanded and updated edition contains 12 complete do-it-yourself tours with information on Chassidic neighborhoods, the Lower East Side, historic landmark synagogues, mikvehs, and Jewish entertainment.

Paperback 200 pages $8.50

Oscar Israelowitz's
Guide to Jewish New York City

LECTURE PROGRAMS

by
Oscar Israelowitz

The Wandering Jews of New York City

The Synagogues of Europe

The Synagogues of the United States

The Source of the Synagogue - Synagogues of Israel

Synagogues Around the World

The multi-media programs (lecture, slide presentation, and sound track) are available for your special organizational meetings. For further information please write to:

Lectures
c/o Mr. Oscar Israelowitz
P.O. Box 228
Brooklyn, New York 11229

(718) 951 - 7072

GUIDED TOURS
OF THE
LOWER EAST SIDE

- Visit the "old neighborhood"..
- Explore Orchard Street...
- See historic synagogues...
- Enjoy wine-tasting in a kosher wine cellar...

FOR FURTHER INFORMATION &
RESERVATIONS CALL
(718) 951-7072
Oscar Israelowitz

Index

Photographic Credits

Temple Emanu-El *11, 12*
Spring Hill Avenue Temple *13, 14, 15*
Temple Beth Or *15, 16, 17, 18, 19*
American Jewish Historical Society *28, 97, 131*
Romer Collection, Miami Public Library *31, 32*
Congregation Ahavath Chesed *34, 35*
The American Hebrew *63*
Congregation Children of Israel *65*
Congregation Mickve Israel *68, 69*
Touro Synagogue *76*
Louisiana State Archives *90, 91*
Congregation Beth Elohim *106, 107, 108, 109*
Congregation Ohabai Sholom *121, 122*
National Museum of American Jewish History *128, 129*
Adath Jeshurun Synagogue *132*
United Federation of Tidewater *135, 136, 137*
Congregation Beth Ahabah *139*
American Jewish Archives *147*
Temple Shalom *148*

BIOGRAPHICAL SKETCH

Born in Brussels, Belgium, Mr. Oscar Israelowitz brings a rich background to his mission of documenting Jewish neighborhoods. He is a professional architect and photographer. Among his noted architectural projects are the Synagogue and Holocaust Center of the Bobover Chassidim in Borough Park and the Yeshiva Rabbi Chaim Berlin (elementary school) in the Flatbush section of Brooklyn. He has also designed several homes and villas in the United States, Haiti, and Israel. He has exhibited his photographs in museums throughout the New York area, including the Brooklyn and Whitney Museums. Mr. Israelowitz has appeared on several television and radio programs including NBC's *First Estate - Religion In Review.* Mr. Israelowitz gives lectures on various Jewish travel topics and has now expanded his walking and bus tours of Jewish neighborhoods to Jewish boat tours around Manhattan and a series of Jewish Heritage Tours of the Caribbean and Eastern and Western Europe.

NOTES

NOTES

NOTES

NOTES

NOTES

NOTES

NOTES

NOTES

NOTES

NOTES

NOTES

NOTES

NOTES

NOTES

NOTES

NOTES